WITHDRAWN

When Whites Riot

When Whites Riot

WRITING RACE AND VIOLENCE
IN AMERICAN AND
SOUTH AFRICAN CULTURES

Sheila Smith McKoy

The University of Wisconsin Press

The University of Wisconsin Press
1930 Monroe Street
Madison, Wisconsin 53711

www.wisc.edu/wisconsinpress/

3 Henrietta Street
London WC2E 8LU, England

1   3   5   4   2

Printed in the United States of America

Library of Congress Cataloging-in-Publication Data
Smith McKoy, Sheila.
When whites riot : writing race and violence
in American and South African cultures / Sheila Smith McKoy.
182 pp.   cm.
Includes bibliographical references and index.
ISBN 0-299-17390-9 (alk.: paper)
ISBN 0-299-17394-1 (pbk.: alk. paper)
1. United States—Race relations.   2. Whites—United States—History
3. Riots—United States—History.   4. Racism—United States.
5. Mass media and race relations—United States.
6. South Africa—Race relations.   7. Whites—South Africa—History
8. Riots—South Africa—History.   9. Racism—South Africa.
10. Mass media and race relations—South Africa.   I. Title.
E184.A1 S664   2001
305.8'00968—dc21   2001002077

For

the millions who have died as a result of racial violence
whose sacrifice must not be forgotten

my father, Raymond Smith, Jr.,
whose spirit will always guide me

my great uncle, Alfonso Faison,
whose memory inspires me

my son, Raymond Smith McKoy,
whose love and wisdom have always humbled me

Contents

vii

Illustrations

Acknowledgments

Several people have been instrumental and inspirational to me during my research for this book. The debt that I owe to many of them can never be repaid. Cathy Davidson, Elizabeth Mudimbe-Boyi, Susan Willis, and so many others at Duke University inspired me to transform my obsession into a book. It would be impossible to thank Karla F. C. Holloway enough for her incredible insight, for her theoretical rigor, and for her presence in my life. My brother and colleague, Mongezi Guma, provided insightful critique of the project even as his heart and mind were understandably focused on South Africa. Victor Anderson, Lewis V. Baldwin, Francis Nii-Amoo Dodoo, and H. R. Houston not only offered me their unconditional support but also gave generously of their time. I am fortunate to have also had the support of Keith Clark, Tracy Iyesha Atkins, and the late J. W. Morrison. Thanks is also due to Jack and Angelina Mthenjane, who allowed me to walk with them through their memories of Soweto 1976.

I am indebted as well to my friends and colleagues at Vanderbilt University whose wisdom and experience have been much appreciated. Vanderbilt University also provided institutional support through research fellowships that enabled me to complete this project. The Special Collections librarians at Fisk University, Ann Allan Shockley and Beth Howse, made the time I spent completing primary research on the Chesnutt chapter a pleasure. This project also would not have been possible without the support of the excellent staffs of the Cape Fear Museum, the North Carolina Department of Archives and History, and the Wilmington Public Library. I also appreciate the assistance of the members of St. Mark's Episcopal Church of Wilmington and Marilyn Raider of AP/Wide World Photos. I am grateful to Gwenn Branche, John Berard, Simone Wilson, and Groesbeck Parharm who assisted me at critical times during my research.

I would also like to thank my readers from the University of Wisconsin

Press for not only seeing my vision but also for their generous comments. Raphael Kadushin's unwavering support of my project made it a reality. Sheila McMahon, the most patient editorial assistant I know, made the difficulties of the publication process seem easy to overcome. I owe much to Juliet Skuldt for her careful and almost painless editing of the manuscript.

Although I could never really find the right words with which to do so, I would like to thank my son, Raymond S. McKoy, who gave so generously of his time and his encouragement from the inception of this book. Finally, I thank my family—Mary Smith Morrison, Patsy Smith Morgan, Christopher Smith, Linda Smith, James Reginald Morrison, Michael Morgan, and Tonya Morrison—each of whom has been my inspiration.

When Whites Riot

Introduction

White Riot—Binding American and
South African Cultures

"Don't let it touch me! the blackness! Lord!" he whispered to any handy
angle in the sky.

—Gwendolyn Brooks, "Riot"

. . . only the blond colossus vomits its indigestible black stepchildren like
autotoxins.

—Arthur Nortje, "Autopsy"

W hat does it mean that at the close of every century—and increasingly at the end of every decade—we question the racial contours
of society, focusing on the ways in which race functions as a cultural tro-
pism? Indeed, what national contours are shaped by the idea of race, especially in America and South Africa, which are themselves national bodies
defined by the idea of racial difference and white supremacy? In the United
States and South Africa, these questions take on vastly different shapes de-
pending upon the racial context of the questioners. Despite centuries of de-
bating race, cultural borders in these nations—and in the countries touched
by their economic and social visions—are marked by abiding ideas about
racial difference and white supremacy. And since time is reckoned differently across these race-based boundaries of culture, markers of its passage
signal vastly different things. For people who embrace white supremacy
and its attendant privileges, the endings of decades, centuries, and millen-
nia prompt discussions of societal failures, of technological treacheries, of
expanding and uncontrollable populations of racial "others," of a disquiet-
ness that signals an impending apocalypse.

Such moments signal a single question for the racially marked in America and South Africa: Why does racism and its attendant constructions of the black body continue to shape culture? This is the question that Charles Chesnutt asked at the end of the nineteenth century when he dared to write about the color line in American culture. A century later this same anxiety underpins Rodney King's famous rhetorical question, "Can we all just get along?"[1] Indeed, it is no accident that twentieth-century American culture can be characterized by W. E. B. DuBois's theories of race at its nascent and the neo-Nazi call for racial separation at its close. Not surprisingly, the identical question characterizes the protests against the multiracist policies in apartheid South Africa lodged by Ruth First, Nelson Mandela, Steve Biko, Chris Hani, and their multicoloured South African compatriots—those named and unnamed—whose protests often ended in their deaths. And in the postapartheid era, South Africa attempts to recast its new democracy by insisting on a policy of nonracialism even as it struggles with the economic, educational, physiological, and psychological disparity that is the progeny of its policies of racial separation and black genocide. It is a question to which Americans and South Africans hopelessly return, especially when the idea of race with its insistence on the oppositional relationship between whiteness and blackness erupts in racial violence. These very difficult questions shape my inquiry into the relationship between culture, race, and violence in *When Whites Riot*.

These dual and forever dueling discourses in America and South Africa are mired in a cultural mindset that enacts whiteness as privilege, thereby solidifying the cultural positions from which these two question sets arise. To interrogate the state of race relations is, in fact, to question every facet of the national cultures of the United States and South Africa. Invariably, such discussion will eventually focus on the idea of *race*'s most volatile social manifestation: race riots. For this reason, *When Whites Riot* seeks to encourage a dialogue that will forever change the way we read the phenomenon of race riot. *When Whites Riot* interrogates the relationships between race, ethnicity, culture, and nationalism in order to uncover the ways in which these concepts shape our reading of the riot act. While I understand the postmodern impulse with its concern about ontology beyond the limitations of "race," "culture," and "nationalism," it is a fact that in American and South African cultures, whiteness has a significant social value that makes racial violence always proximate and always self-prolegomenous. Readers familiar with the debates about Afrocentricity, Eurocentricity, and the like should realize that the fact that race riots continue to define the state of race (mis)relations in these cultures makes our *theoretical* assumptions about these issues seem hopelessly ineffectual. It is, after all, impossible to theorize away the existence of racial violence.

In the United States and South Africa, race riots are always imagined as violence involving black people, of black bodies perpetually defined and affected by violence. In essence, race riots are framed as events involving only the violent and violating black bodies that are the ultimate markers of racial difference. Race riots, then, demonstrate the reason why—to borrow Cornel West's phraseology—race matters. However, as *When Whites Riot* reveals, racial violence is often—indeed, perhaps most often—enacted by white bodies that represent the violent embrace of white racial domination. As Jacques Derrida so adeptly observes, apartheid haunts American and South African cultures in similar ways.[2] And as this work seeks to demonstrate, white riot is one of the cultural practices that equate the relationship between America's racial melting pot and both South Africa's apartheid state and her nonracial one. This study is designed to exorcise the demon of blackness imposed on these incidents of racial violence. *When Whites Riot* explores white racial violence—those events that have been misnamed as "race riots"—to expose the ways in which race and violence are integral to American and South African cultures.

Although it should be clear by now, I want to insist on the existence of the causal relationship between white privilege and racial violence because white riots occur in racialized societies, places in which blackness is constructed as being alien to the cultural norm. These oppositions are encoded in the valance of white supremacy, which both engenders violence and depends upon it to maintain the racial divides that white supremacy claims. In practice, then, racial violence is never read as a white phenomenon. Media portraits of riot events are montages of people of color and, in particular, black people (and it is important to note that in the United States and South Africa, white is not imagined in terms of color) who become dangerous abstractions when racial violence erupts. This conflation of violence and blackness, as Karla Holloway notes, is a part of the pattern of institutionalized racism.[3] However, racial violence involving whites is never identified as a riot even in the face of historical and documentary evidence that exposes them as such.[4] In this context white riot is validated and characterized as "rebellion," "civil duty," "revolution," or the like because the cultural tempers of the United States and South Africa have already prefigured racial violence as a black act. It remains difficult even to conceive of the idea of a white racial riot. My objective in the chapters that follow is to limn the phenomena of white riot by exploring specific moments of racial violence that have been historically looked at as race riots.

When Whites Riot comments on the incredible synergy between the privileges of whiteness and racial violence. It claims the necessity to identify white riots by examining the literary, historical, and documentary evidence of selected riot events that, having been read through the racialized lenses of American and South African cultures, have been filed under the various misnomers of "race riots," "racial uprisings," and "black rebellions."

This work addresses the ways in which these two "apartheid" cultures not only sanction racialized violence but also reproduce riot events in the guise of black violent insurgency. *When Whites Riot* analyzes four episodes of white riot chronologically: the Wilmington Race Riot of 1898; the Soweto Uprising of 1976; the Los Angeles Rebellion of 1992; and the Mmabatho, Bophuthatswana, Election Riots of 1994. My linking of these temporal and national moments is neither haphazard nor arbitrary. Despite the differences in time and place, these episodes reveal that white riots cannot be explained away by analyzing how power, race, and violence operate at a single historical moment. Each episode is figured as a race riot because the idea of blackness in these cultures has been used to sanction the racial hierarchies that inform South African and American cultures. Remembering these events as race riots functions to keep race at the center of the social consciousness of these nations; it is an example of what Homi Bhabha identifies as the double writing of a racial cultural liminality within these nations.[5] As I demonstrate in *When Whites Riot*, these episodes of racial unrest are actually white riots which erupt in similar ways in both nations, so persistently, in fact, that they span a millennium. The white riots at the center of these events have been ruthlessly erased (and raced) at the discretion of the hegemony.

When Whites Riot, therefore, is not a genealogy about how race riot is placed along a continuum of rebellion, revolution, or insurgency. Instead, the guiding premise of this study is to make white riots as visible as the racialized violence they incite. The project as a whole focuses on the representations of race riots in the United States and in apartheid and postapartheid South Africa, nations linked by the structure and practice of white supremacy. The process of defining the events in Wilmington, Soweto, Los Angeles, and Mmabatho as race riots is dependent upon cultural assumptions that superimpose blackness on the riot scene as a convenient means of reinscribing the privileges associated with whiteness.

In the episodes of racial violence that *When Whites Riot* examines, black bodies remain at the center of each white riot, both claimed and blamed by the same set of hegemonic practices. This dislocation allows for the kinds of slippages that enable the historical record to focus on black bodies in the midst of the violence, while erasing the white bodies that instigate and initiate the violence. My task here is to identify the cultural biases that make white riot invisible in these apartheid states and to render these events, and the cultural assumptions that make them possible, accessible to broader cultural critique. To that end, *When Whites Riot* focuses on the cultural practices that blanket white riot by covering it with the cultural "normative" of *race riot*.

The genesis of this work is rooted in both personal and intellectual obsessions, based on events that led to my present understanding of the commonality between American and South African cultures. In June 1976, at the time of the Soweto riots, I had just graduated from high school in the midst of America's bicentennial celebration. Far from the life and death struggles endured by the students in Soweto at that time, my classmates and I had protested against an administration that was opposed to outward demonstrations of "black pride" during what was then known as "Black History Week." That spring, my black classmates and I were a part of what the local paper had claimed were "race riots," despite the fact that we had mounted a nonviolent demonstration. The fact that our actions were described as a "race riot" was based solely on the ways in which our bodies were read by a culture familiar with the association of our blackness with violence. That bicentennial moment was also the time during which I "discovered" (a term I use here in the tradition of the discursive foundations of European colonization) that North Carolina had been the scene of one of the most atrocious events of racial violence in the history of the nation: the Wilmington Race Riot of 1898. By the time these personal discoveries had become intellectual obsessions, the racial violence that yet again summoned the riots, this time in Los Angeles, and the coverage of the riots in the national press, was as predictable as the events and coverage of the Mmabatho election violence that occurred so proximately to it. In both instances, the battered black bodies "explained" the scenes of racial violence that were introduced—albeit offstage according to the news coverage of these events—by white racial violence. *When Whites Riot* is the culmination of all of these moments of discovery.

The specific intersection of race and riot in cultures that are clearly racialized is what unites this study of Wilmington, Soweto, Los Angeles, and Mmabatho. And critical to my reading of these white riots is the way in which media (and mediated) images of the violence and news coverage of the events respond to white riot. Also integral to my process of *discovering* the white riots in each of these episodes of racial violence is the role that both historical fiction and oral narratives play in making white riot visible. My focus in each of the chapters that follow is to track both the process of blanketing white riot in press accounts and the process of unmasking white riot in fictionalized and oral recoveries of the riot events. The first chapter, "Riot-Making: Ululation, Resistance, and Reclamation," is an examination of how race riots are made and perpetuated by the desire to reinforce and reinscribe the existing social order. In this chapter I focus on the concept of white racialized ululation, the call to violence that incites white riots.

Chapter 2, "Reading the Riot Act: The Teleology of Charles Chesnutt's *The Marrow of Tradition* and the Wilmington Race Riot of 1898," is an exploration of the events surrounding what is popularly known as the "Wilmington Race Riot" of 1898.[6] In addition to examining how the violence is designed and initiated by the white minority in Wilmington, I trace the methodology of Chesnutt's revisioning of the historical record of riot in the novel. In particular I emphasize the extent to which Chesnutt is able to unmask the history of the white riot in Wilmington, despite the fact that the novel was published only three years after the event.

Chapter 3, "Rioting in a State of Siege: The Cultural Contexts of Sipho Sepamla's *A Ride on the Whirlwind* and the Soweto Uprising of 1976," explores the construction of racialized violence during the aftermath of what has been (mis)identified as the Soweto Uprising. My focus here is on the ways in which white riot is affected by the emergence of a black consciousness in a culture where the empowered minority insists that black consciousness cannot exist. And since the social power of the Afrikaner minority also hinges on the "denaturalization" of black South Africans, this chapter is also a commentary on how the riot event is influenced by white resistance to black cultural belongingness. I examine Sipho Sepamla's account of the 1976 riot aftermath in *A Ride on the Whirlwind* and visual adaptations of the violence in the films *Sarafina!* and *Cry Freedom*.[7]

Chapter 4, "Subverting the Silences: Historicizing White Riot in Fiction and Film," is an extended reading of the ways in which white riot is constructed in both literary and film texts. This chapter identifies the ways in which white riot is silenced in the discourse of both American and South African cultures. Finally, the epilogue, "The Tie That Binds—Los Angeles and Mmabatho, White Riot on the Cusp of a New Millennium," centers on the cultural legacy of white riot. My emphasis here is on the ways in which the riot texts of Los Angeles 1992 and in Mmabatho 1994 reflect the historical moment as harbingers of the cultural violence to come. My ideas here are confirmed in the almost mirror-image discourses of President Bill Clinton's Initiative on Race and South Africa's Truth and Reconciliation

Commission. The coincidence of their respective publications further connect the ways in which America and South Africa are and will continue to be plagued by racial violence as long as both cultures continue to frame race as a phantasm and racial violence as the manifestation of its haunting. Through these reflections *When Whites Riot* seeks to perform a critical investigation of the collision of race, violence, and culture in these racially complex national spaces.

1

Riot-Making

Ululation, Resistance, and Reclamation

Our appeal is to the white men with white hearts, who love their race
better than they love pie. They compose the rank and file of the white men
of all parties. They want decent government. They are tired of the scandals,
elevation of the negro, and the outrages that characterize the present rule.
They are laying aside party lines and coming together to restore White
Supremacy.
—Democratic Broadside, North Carolina, United States, 1898

A critical component of a constructive and honest national dialogue about
race and racism is a greater public awareness of the history of oppression,
conquest, and private and government-sanctioned discrimination and their
present-day consequences. Fundamental to this historical understanding is
an appreciation of the ways in which the long history of slavery in this
country has codified the system of racial hierarchy in which white privilege
has been protected by custom and then by law.
—The President's Initiative on Race Advisory Board, *One America in the 21st
Century,* 1998

You have only to sacrifice the "nigger" absolutely and the game is easy.
Deep down in the heart of every Dutchman in South Africa is the ideal of a
white land-owning aristocracy resting on slave labour (of course, the word
"slave" here is carefully eschewed, nor do they exactly want slaves, but
simply the cheap labour of the black proletariat without any rights of any
sort or kind).
—Sir Alfred Milner, 1899

Through apartheid, the white community retained political and
economic power. The unequal distribution of resources meant that white
communities benefited through well-serviced suburbs, accessible education,
access to government and other employment opportunities, and countless
other advantages. Whilst only a minority of white people engaged in the

direct perpetration of violence, many gross human rights violations were
committed in order to retain these benefits.
          —*The Truth and Reconciliation Commission of South Africa Report,* 1998

I n the fall of 1998 something extraordinary happened in the United States
and South Africa. Both governments, the latter under the leadership of
the first black South African president, Nelson Mandela, published official documents characterizing the state of race relations in their respective
countries. South Africa's Truth and Reconciliation Commission published
its findings in the same year that the United States government issued *One
America in the 21st Century,* the report of President Bill Clinton's Initiative on Race. Both documents admit their nation's historical acceptance of
white privilege, a system that has been largely maintained by racial violence. In these significant documents, both governments confess that white
privilege and racial violence underpin their national discourses. Understanding the place racial violence holds in the United States and South
Africa is a critical part of my work on white riot, the incendiary nature of
it, and hence, the threat its absence poses to the idea of nationhood in what
are clearly countries defined by the specter of apartheid. Fundamentally,
then, the link between racial violence and white privilege both determines
and is determined by the idea of blackness in these apartheid states.

    Interestingly enough, despite the fact that both *The Truth and Recon-
ciliation Commission of South Africa Report* and *One America in the 21st Century* associate violence with white privilege, racial violence historically has
been blamed on people of color in both the United States and South Africa.
In other words, when race is coupled with violence, the national inclination
is to blacken the violence, even when that violence victimizes communities
of color. This is possible because "race" is configured around the black and
colored bodies upon which white privilege is sustained. Now that racial
violence has been claimed as a means of maintaining white privilege in the
United States and South Africa, it is important to understand the ways in
which this relationship is replicated through a complex system of societal
norms, a variety of media, and the images generated in the popular culture.

    In the face of this evidence, it is clearly not coincidental that race riots
and uprisings (another name for violent actions that, like race riots, are centered in black and other communities of color) are perpetually associated
with violent and violating black bodies in South Africa and the United
States. That is, through the resources afforded to white privilege in these

apartheid spaces, white racial violence is covered by the images of race riots, of the black and violent bodies that must be controlled in order to sustain the social order. My task in this chapter is to identify the process through which white violence becomes colorized as black insurgency, a process that is replicated in each of the episodes of racial violence I discuss in this book.

In American and South African cultures, the power of race is inscribed through a variety of methods: the interpretation of sacred texts, the written and visual cues used in the news media, color-coded language, political discourse, in essence, through all the ways in which culture is written. White privilege, then, replicates itself through all these cultural sites because of South Africa's and America's simultaneous insistence on maintaining a racial hierarchy while also maintaining the social order. Michael Parenti describes this process as attribution, the process of constructing social positions as if they are equally assessable to everyone. In the United States the process of attribution insists that everyone has equal access to opportunity. In South Africa attribution legitimizes the notion that different social positions represent the "natural order of things."[1] In apartheid South Africa, the natural social order was plainly written in a chain of being that placed black South Africans on the bottom—economically, socially, and politically—and placed white South Africans at the zenith. This legacy is so persistent, in fact, that in postapartheid South Africa Mandela has reminded white South Africans that they have to be willing to share the wealth in this country where black poverty has continued to be the primary social problem. In both places attribution allows for a construction of "whiteness" that ignores class boundaries, allowing for the natural ordering of society along a unified, white racial line. Whiteness, then, is mythologized as an identity without real class borders. Political, economic, and social institutions replicate this notion, making the adversative seem normal.

The press, of course, plays a vital role in the dissemination of the race ideology that arises from this situation and contributes to riot events. As Noam Chomsky notes, the press produces and uses the illusions that are necessary to "contain the domestic enemy."[2] Two decades before Chomsky addressed this issue, Malcolm X, defined by the press as perhaps the representative domestic enemy of his era, described this process as the power of the press to make the American people love or hate at will. In each of the riot incidents that I examine here, these "illusions" make racialized violence seem both necessary and unavoidable. This kind of racial façade is the reason that every episode of white riot is hidden by a "race riot" that

The remains of William Brown, who was beaten, shot, and burned at the Douglas County Courthouse in Omaha, Nebraska, 28 September 1919 (Photograph courtesy of the Nebraska State Historical Society)

dominates media images of racial violence. And these images often revolve around scenes of segregated neighborhoods and the dangers of unregulated social access. These scenes are never of the images from "next door," and this distance, especially the racial distance implied by these images, is comforting. Marked by the manipulation of contrasting symbols of the oppressor and the oppressed—and in the discourse of white supremacy, whites are the ones targeted for oppression—these images prefigure the inevitability of racial violence.

These racial associations, based on the archetypes assigned by white supremacist thought, inform readings of riot events. Clearly, not all group violence becomes figured as a "race riot"; however, any event named by the hegemony as a "race riot" is always colorized. In effect, group violence is identified differently when the participants are not people of color. Violence that cannot escape being identified with rioting white bodies is sanctioned by apartheid societies. A cursory glance at the historical documentation of "lynching bees," "stands," or other such actions for the "public good" portray white racial violence as a political and social necessity. Racial violence, then, is treated according to the identity of the riot participants. My focus on the ways in which race and violence inform culture in the United States and South Africa limns the contours of this mutual national divide.

ACCULTURATING RACIAL VIOLENCE: THE LEGACY
OF APARTHEID IN THE UNITED STATES AND SOUTH AFRICA

Despite the tendency to distance race relationships in the United States from the notions associated with race in South Africa, the term apartheid appropriately describes the racialized culture of the United States. As Toni Morrison insists, the American cultural and historical "condition [is] a racially articulated and predicated world."[3] And there is more than enough evidence to suggest that South African apartheid owes its racial structure to the system of segregation that defined the United States prior to the Civil Rights movement. Regardless of the fact that South African apartheid is couched as being more extreme than the system of racial hierarchy at play in America, the same race dynamics are indeed at work in both spaces. Maurice Evans's *Black and White in South East Africa* (which, incidentally, had to be published by a "negro" press in order to find editorial support) details the historical elements of this connection.[4] And John Cell, writing in *The Highest Stage of White Supremacy,* points out that the link between these spaces is not accidental. In fact, he notes that "South Africans of all races watched the American case closely and made it a germane, though not a determining, part of their own discussion."[5] George Fredrickson also argues that there is some basis for comparison, although he notes that southern blacks, whom he sees as the primary targets of American apartheid, were recognized as citizens and not as alien to American society.[6] However, as I have already indicated, the racing of the black body in America is tantamount to being cast as alien despite the geographical location of the bodies targeted. The ways in which racial bodies are read in South Africa and in the United States are related precisely because, as Jacques Derrida observes, American and South African cultures are shaped by their similar relationships to the racial "hell" of apartheid.[7]

I acknowledge that there are distinct differences between these cultures; in fact, the cultural similitude in the shape of the black body politic in South Africa and the United States is all the more powerful because of the significant differences in their national histories. Moreover, these societies have habitually and continually reflected each other in reference to the cultural racing of the black body. In "Minding South Africa," Lewis Nkosi, a black South African who wrote primarily as an exile, calls attention to

Sparks's "preoccupation with the history of African Americans." Nkosi's discussion of Allister Sparks's *The Mind of South Africa* prompts him to consider what Sparks must have seen of the "obvious parallels which can be drawn between the American and the African Souths."[8] Yet the cultural connections surpass a mere preoccupation with geographic declination. As Rob Nixon suggests, there has been a significant amount of the creative interplay between black writers in the United States and South Africa.[9] Undeniably, there are linguistic, cultural, and ideological references that these two nations share despite their particularized national histories.

It is because of their similitude in the promulgation of race ideology and white privilege that American and South African cultures share, for example, the terminology of race and racial division. Although the linkages are far too significant and complex to simply list, there are some notable cultural intersections that shape my exploration of white riot. Black people are "niggerized" in both spaces, a linguistic phenomenon that is rooted in the slave histories that the United States and South Africa have in common. The term *colored* in the United States, though no longer in popular usage, interestingly parallels the racial situation of the mixed-race "coloureds" in South Africa. This connection is certainly made visible by the fact that the minstrel tradition, an undeniably American tradition—complete with its stereotypical costuming and racial masking—thrives in South Africa amongst its coloured population. Significantly, racial designations and divisions that were legally enforced in South Africa during the apartheid era were socially and often violently enforced in the United States. Some of these divisions—including segregated cemeteries, churches, and neighborhoods—persist in the United States and continue to be a factor even in the "new" South Africa.[10] Although these social connections are addressed in the literature of both cultures, other discourses are largely silent about these connections.[11] The balance of power in both nations thus depends upon replicating the binary opposition of blackness and whiteness that lies at the root of white supremacy.

It is also clear that when this opposition is threatened, there are ways in which American and South African cultural systems use each other to reinscribe white supremacy. For instance, at the height of the Civil Rights movement in the United States, Hollywood refused to accurately portray images of black protest in the films of the era; indeed, the idea of racial difference had always been problematic—and therefore ripe for dependence upon negative stereotyping—in the Hollywood imagination which is, after all, one of the ways in which America imagines itself. Instead, Hollywood turned to South Africa to reproduce images of white supremacy and black subjugation on more comfortable racial terrain. A telling example of this racial chiasmus occurred when *Cry, the Beloved Country* was filmed in 1951, just three years after apartheid became the law of the land in South Africa. All of the black members of the cast, including Canada Lee and Sidney Poitier, were admitted into the country as Bantu laborers in the employ of the director.[12] This adaptation of Alan Patton's novel depicts an image of South Africa in which the victims of apartheid are tried and found guilty of its consequences. The narrative revolves around the murder trial of a black South African who is accused of killing a white man who had dedicated his life to the ideals of racial equality. Found guilty—and admittedly so—the defendant is hanged for the crime of murder under the justice of the apartheid regime which remains blameless and intact.

At this time the racial situation in the United States was highly charged. Race riots and lynchings dominated the news. African Americans were actively agitating for equal rights in housing and equal access to education and public transportation. In fact, just prior to the year *Cry, the Beloved Country* was filmed in South Africa, two different petitions were submitted to the United Nations charging the United States with human rights violations against its black citizens, including charges of black genocide.[13] When *Cry, the Beloved Country* was filmed, black agency in the United States was certainly not as palatable to the American racial tastes of the era as were the racial difficulties pictured in *Cry, the Beloved Country*. Despite the film's obvious appeal for the plight of black South Africans, the protagonist is ultimately at the mercy of an apartheid regime. Interestingly, by the time the film was remade and released in 1995, America was attempting to recover from the Rodney King–inspired riots that shook Los Angeles and many other urban centers. The cultural power of the relationship between these apartheid states is also one of the reasons that American corporations resisted divesting in South Africa when it was the focus of international sanctions. It should not be surprising, then, that the United States was also one of the principal countries to which white South Africans immigrated as it became clear that the apartheid government was about to collapse.

American and South African notions about race are traceable through numerous disciplines and are spawned by what V. Y. Mudimbe refers to as "an already too well-known evolutionary hallucination."[14] It is not my intention to replicate the body of work that has already been the subject of significant scholarly attention; Mudimbe as well as other African and African diaspora theorists have already examined the limits of these theories.[15] Moreover, numerous treatises have exposed the relative powerlessness of reading the black body as being physiologically, biologically, or intellectually different from white bodies. My point is that however limited the theory, the black body at the center of the debate is made vulnerable to effects of power based on white "apprehension" of blackness. As the incidents of racial violence in Wilmington, Soweto, Los Angeles, and Mmabatho reveal, the fact that these cultures reproduce *white riots* as *race riots* signals their cultural similitude even in the face of cultural histories that should deny, rather than support, their racial resemblance.

WHITE RIOT/RACE RIOT: REFLECTIONS IN THE MIRROR
OF WHITE SUPREMACY

In as much as the apartheid cultures of the United States and South Africa have a great deal in common, the riot act and the signifying black bodies that accompany this kind of violence are clearly framed in the literature, media, and films of these nations in similar ways. Language and the cultural construction of racial identities are at the center of how riot is figured in these apartheid states. In every available representative space from literature to the popular culture, and through a variety of visual media, race riots are represented in terms of the threat they pose to the social order. Such representations perpetually insure the necessity of white riot. A white riot, then, cannot be reduced to the incendiary moment at which the violence erupts because the disempowered have also embraced violence as the only response to such situations; nor can white riot be considered separately from the social privileges it is designed to maintain. In South Africa and the United States, threats to the hegemony are always packaged in black bodies. Focusing on the black body, these societies produce race riots around the image of blackness that is a part of the ideology of race in that culture. This reading of the black body is at the center of the violence in each of the episodes of riot I shall discuss. And this dislocation allows for the kinds of slippages that must take place to enable the historical record to focus on black bodies in the midst of racial violence while erasing the white bodies that so often initiate the violence.

In Wilmington in 1898, for instance, what has been misnamed as a "race riot" was manipulated by members of the Democratic Party, which was then a "lily-white" organization, as part of a political coup designed to reinscribe the political domination of the their party. The manipulation I describe is not an antiseptic process of articulating the possibility or plausibility of violence. The riot began not with black aggression, but with the movement of the local white militia led by prominent white citizens into a black neighborhood. Armed with a Gatling gun, these men opened fire on a black population that had literally and systematically been denied access to weapons. Yet the historical record reads this event in terms of rioting black bodies at its center, as a "race riot," rather than as the white riot it was.

A set of similar interactions precedes the violence in Soweto in 1976 where, in keeping with the twentieth-century version of the white riot, the white rioters were police officers. This was true of Soweto and was certainly also true of the prelude to the racial violence in Los Angeles during the 1992 unrest. The violence in Los Angeles that followed the verdicts to acquit the police officers involved in the King incident was the prolegomenon; the beating was itself a white riot, despite the presence of the officers of color who were clearly subordinate to the officers whose riotous actions sparked the costliest riots in American history. In each of these incidents rioting white bodies filled the scene, yet they were replaced with renderings of black violence. How this slippage occurs is a part of the legacy of race in the United States and South Africa; it is a function of the systems of white privilege that they share. As Cornel West indicates, one of the ways that race operates is to legitimize the idea of white supremacy.[16] In his move to uncomplicate what is behind the discourse of white supremacy and black displacement, West focuses on the fact that white supremacy is authorized by disciplines that read black bodies socially, rather than scientifically. The black body, then, is conceived of as both alien and unequal. This correlation persists in the racialized spaces of South Africa and the United States. Central to my analysis is the extent to which this notion of white supremacy racializes these spaces. It is what allowed black Africans, who comprised nearly 80 percent of the population of apartheid South Africa, to be in the position of having to demand their rights from white South Africans, who comprised about 12 percent of the population. This same dynamic enabled white domination of the South during Reconstruction, when the South was also predominately black. The way white supremacy literally makes race shaped the social situation that erupted into the Wilmington race riot. This same cultural archetype allowed for the legal creation of black townships in South Africa and the manipulated segregation of black neighborhoods—that literally existed on the other side of the railroad tracks—in America. My look at white riot, then, also necessarily addresses the larger problem of the way in which race shapes culture in the United States and South Africa.

When white privilege defines the national culture, the black body is articulated in terms of differences that, though based on the idea of color, suggest an abiding difference underneath the skin. This idea of difference is based in Western philosophical constructions of blackness that, for instance, provided Kant with enough information to posit a racial hierarchy in which the black race is placed on the bottom. That Kant's construction of racial hierarchy is problematic is certainly obvious given that, like the apprehension of blackness in South African and American national discourses, it is an outgrowth of an imagination polluted by white privilege. And although Anthony Appiah continually sets aside the notions of morphology and phenotype in reference to race, it is clear that any trace of blackness is sufficient to inform the notion of racial difference in these apartheid spaces. Even in the absence of these morphological markers, blackness is imbued with a tenacity that colorizes the social space, especially when racial violence occurs. There is no mediating space in which blackness survives without being associated with violence. Indeed, for those who might claim to bridge the racial gap between black and white — including people of color who embrace the ideals of white supremacy — there is no possibility of compromise. In short, there is no position of perfect "Clarence Thomasian" order that allows for any exceptions in the way in which blackness is read in an apartheid context. It is not a matter of cultural difference that sustains both America's embrace of her melting pot ideology *and* her equal inability to move beyond racial designation and racist action; it is a matter of what race means in America. Likewise, South African culture, with its movement from a multiethnic/racial culture to the new nonracial culture still reels from the reality of racist practice; the school integration riots of the postapartheid era are simply the latest event in a progression of culturally racist phenomena. Racist practice quite simply thrives in the face of cultural integration, and it tenaciously discounts the idea of "racelessness." In the face of such tenacity it is clear that much theoretical work must be done to make white riot visible.

The term *race riot* creates a powerful cultural space in apartheid places; it is applied to any action of protest, violent or nonviolent, that originates in the disempowered community. This space, after all, is where all riots, white or otherwise, begin. "Rioters" by their very choice of action attempt to assert that the cultural space is their own. They assert that they will continue to participate in the renegotiation of the social order. I want to insist on the fact that the white empowered do become rioters in these instances. They are rioters in the denotative sense of the word, intent upon maintaining white cultural supremacy by any means necessary.

White riot, then, is the point of intersection between ethnicity and race, power and violence.[17] It is veiled by the ways in which apartheid cultures construct images of "race riots" and the fantasy of "noble" white racial violence. White riot is valorized because it is presented as a means to interrupt a cycle of social devolution, one that threatens to destabilize existing class and power structures. The sterilization of such violence is effected by the erasure of blame through linguistic constructions, a process I will delineate later, and the creation of the notion that racial violence perpetrated on the powerless is both necessary and good. It is precisely this interpretation of racial violence that presumes to excuse the white riots represented in this book.

In South Africa, indeed across the African continent, the violence of colonization is sterilized in terms of *settling* and *salvation*. The ideology of settling required the manufacture of an image of white South Africans who themselves become victimized by the abuse of the colonial enterprises of Holland and Britain gone awry, and the ideology of salvation was never without its erstwhile cohort, capitalism. In the United States, racial violence has its historical base in preventing miscegenation—through lynchings, the violent separation the races, and the like—while the society simultaneously condones white male participation in the creation of an increasingly miscellaneous race of enslaved and/or politically powerless progeny. White supremacy makes white riot *look* black and representations of such riots manipulate public sentiment in order to validate these actions.[18]

The participants in the riots of the 1800s in the United States seem easily definable in terms of race, that is, black bodies in the midst of riot situations for which they were to blame. Hence the use of the term *race riot* easily conflates being non-black with being blameless in the riot event. Yet even a cursory examination of these riot events reveals that they were reactions to events that became cataclysmic due to the percussive violence they answered. In the specific incidents I examine in the following chapters, the violence is initiated by the empowered in order to reinscribe the existing social order. What I wish to convey here is that the nomenclature of "race riot" becomes assigned to an event based on its cultural surroundings; it is not based on its immediate intent or on its result. A true race riot is a prolegomenon, an extended event that anticipates societal disruption or evolution.

However, it is necessary to take more than a cursory look at these riots, for even though the term *race* has been dropped from modern descriptions of riots in racialized societies, the mechanisms of race practice acculturate a mindset which links the idea of riot to a violent black presence. The violence of the empowered may not be as immediately recognizable because the participants are white and because they are supported by the civil authority. The violence of the empowered in the twentieth century is centered in a maze of cultural norms—from petty discrimination to gentrifi-

Two riot police clubbing a coloured man during racial unrest in Cape Town, South Africa, 8 September 1976 (AP/Wide World Photos)

cation, from educational inequity to redlining, from returning to "family values" to inequitable sentencing—each a call to reorient the society in accordance with what are essentially race-based cultural standards. The issue at the core of any riot event, then, is how these calls for change are interpreted. Racial violence occurs in the black community not because riot is a black cultural phenomenon but because the black community is at the center of the cultural maze established by apartheid structures. When whites riot, as this discussion will detail, the violence is structured around the black bodies that are then portrayed as victims of their own violent actions. Based on these cultural misformations, the preoccupation with white supremacy in American and South African cultures blackens even the whitest riot scene.

White riot is a phenomenon that is distinct from other violence. I must foreground this issue because race riots are not a part of the same discussion. Race riots are not conceived in terms of Bakhtin's polyglot and its subsequent effect on ways of figuring the world. Bakhtin's is a discussion about the possibilities of language within a constituent community of Europeans, all "I's" and no "others." Race riots are made from a distinct use of language, constituting an entirely different discourse on power that depends upon the consistent presence of a racial "other." The language that marks race riots depends upon the perpetual insistence on unmitigated racial difference.

To understand the ways in which white riot sustains these cultures, it is crucial to understand how apartheid states construct the black body. I want to begin with an examination of the ways in which apartheid discourse apprehends the black body. The term *apprehension* complicates both the epistemology of blackness and the emotion its presence arouses in these countries. In the chapters that follow, I shall focus on the following questions about the construction of the black body in apartheid society: What are the markings of race that accompany white apprehension of the black body? How do these markers of race erase class and cultural similarities making it impossible to equate race with culture? And finally, is it possible, even in theory, to erase the role race plays in cultural violence?

In the episodes of racial violence that I examine here, black bodies are not only always at the center of the assault, they also center the idea of race as a mitigating concept. And these bodies are perpetually figured in the riot scene whether or not those at the center of the violence are visibly black. The black body, particularly in a racialized society, is (mis)constructed in particular ways. The significance of this social situation, though based on erroneous constructions, is neither imagined nor fabricated. In the Wilmington 1898 race riot, one of the black bodies at the center of the debate was that of Alexander L. Manly. Placed in the middle of the discourse about white female bodies and sexual-racial transgression, Manly's "white" appearance did not alleviate the white racist reading of his blackness. His blackness defined his place in the culture of Wilmington, despite the absence of physical evidence of his race. Like Rodney King's body, which was at the center of the Los Angeles riots in 1992, Manly's "unmarked" body became a sexual and racial icon in Wilmington in 1898; his presence justified the racial assault that facilitated what amounted to a military coup of the municipal government of the city. Unable to return to Wilmington even after the riot ended, Manly was perpetually marked and banished from Wilmington. Rodney King's body was indelibly marked in the racialized society of Los Angeles scarcely a century later; it was as identifiable (and available for police action) as his white Hyundai ultimately became even amid the mass of vehicles that crowd the Los Angeles freeways. In South Africa the bodies of school children were marked by violence as the police presence at the scene of the Soweto Uprising reveals. The bodies of black children substantiated the justification of apartheid so much so that by 1985, children were estimated to comprise 40 percent of black South African detainees imprisoned without trial under the South African Terrorist Act. Their bodies were disposable in the culture primarily because of the persistence of images of black death, particularly after instances of government-sponsored black-on-black violence defined the limited value of black life in apartheid South Africa. The black body is the social text that is written on the political space in every episode of racialized violence in the United States and South Africa. The way in which the black body is constructed in these countries situates Wilmington 1898, Soweto 1976, Los Angeles 1992, and Mmabatho 1994 in the same theoretical space.

FROM ULULATION TO VIOLENCE: THE RITUAL PROCESS
OF WHITE RIOT

White racial violence in both the United States and in South Africa arises out of the construction of a national consciousness centering on black bodies, the contamination of blackness, and the need to control this contamination. Unfortunately, apartheid cultures are structured around a definition of whiteness that needs blackness to exist. In essence, whiteness simply cannot exist without the existence of the contaminating black social space, and white riots have been the primary mechanism through which this racial balance is maintained. White riots are part of a ritual process of engendering violence into the cultural consciousness. This ritual revolves around the ordering of society around race and the construction of the black body in particular ways as I have already noted. However, when the racial balance is threatened, those invested in white privilege call for racial violence. This process of evoking the call to arms is what I conceive of as white racialized ululation.

White racialized ululation calls for a response to threats to the social order and simultaneously valorizes the white riots that it calls forth. Ululation is a ritualized process of vocalizing a response to threats to white supremacist order, of a hyperbolic intensification of the emotions that these threats evoke. In cultures where ululation is a commonly acknowledged practice—notably cultures of color—the vocalization characterizes the communal response of a movement through an emotional outpouring that builds in intensity toward an anticipated end. In the Western connotation of the term, ululation is figured as something that is primitive, as the accompaniment to rituals that mark racial difference. What ululation does, though, is elicit a communal response to a cultural moment by shaping its intensity.[19]

I focus on racialized ululation, then, to call attention both to the inaccuracies implicit in these constructions of racialized violence and to what actually transpires prior to a white riot. In effect, I am turning the process of labeling around, using this kind of ululation to call attention to the ways in which the term has been misunderstood in Western discourse. White racialized ululation is a ritualistic call to violence; it is a *call* to action, rather than a *response* to the rioting black bodies that usually fill the scene, making white riot invisible. In the context of social violence, racialized ululation finds its outlet through a variety of cultural reproductions: in newspapers, on television, in documentaries, on film, on talk radio, through the entire spectrum of popular discourse. It is the process of vocalization through the discourse nexus of the popular culture created for the purpose of eliciting a violent response. Racialized ululation coalesces all calls for active preservation of the existing social order. Plainly, it calls forth white riot that in turn elicits linguistic and violent responses from the disempowered community that become the *race riots* that the white supremacist mirror reflects.

Racial violence, then, centers around the promulgation of events, structured to achieve some desired change of a political or economic nature based on a racial or ethnic standard.[20] This foregrounds the two kinds of riot I attend to in this book: the easily recognizable race riot involving people of color and the easily deniable incidents of white racial violence. White riot and white racialized ululation conflate notions of resistance and power. White rioters intend to subvert resistance to social change; participants in white racialized ululation intend to foreground race and ethnicity to maintain racial stratification and the disproportionate distribution of power that accompanies it. Certainly what is striking about the "race riots" I consider here is that the representations of the riots belie both the savagery of the violence and the locus of the violence. Riots are controlled by the "weaponry" of war: Gatling guns, army and National Guard units, and specially trained riot police. It is a telling commentary that in the United States and South Africa incidents of racial violence are the most horrific kind of cultural violence on record.

A traditional look at race riot, as this book demonstrates, could not begin to examine the true nature of racial violence in the United States and South Africa. Despite the fact that white bodies riot in each of these incidents, such readings commonly associate the violence with black people. These renderings enable the white empowered to resist examining the riot scene in order to disassociate the white race from the riot act itself. This slippage not only allows for the common association of black bodies with rioting but also negotiates ways to control the black populations. Yet as my readings show, this practice informs each of the riot episodes included here; the reenactment is ensured by the racialized societies that both produce and condemn race riot. It is an association based on the repetition of the same cultural practices that culminate in race riots despite the national differences. My task, then, is to disrupt the cultural biases that make white riot invisible in these apartheid states and to render these events accessible to broader cultural critique.

WITNESSING WHITE RIOT: THE NECESSITY OF A LITERARY HISTORY

White riot hides behind an elaborate intrigue in the United States and South Africa. It is an intrigue that has been challenged in a variety of ways in black-centered texts; however, these textual witnesses occupy a space that is complicated by the history of protest expression in the United States and South Africa. The difficulty of discussing white riot lies in the (mis)appropriation of evidence by the empowered; it is, in short, an arduous task to limn white riot. In order to initiate the process of recovery, though, I begin with a look at the ways in which riot is documented in the United States and South Africa.

In the United States the history of riot protest is grounded in the relationship between the black press and African American narrative expression. Although African American poetry existed prior to the first black press, as the experience of Phillis Wheatley in publishing *Poems on Various Subjects, Religious and Moral* (1773) reveals, access to publication was dependent upon white preface. Karla Holloway notes that Wheatley's entrée into the literary world endangered "the codes of judicial conduct that kept black and white lives apart."[21] However, since Wheatley's access to the publishing industry depended upon gaining approval from eighteen white men, Wheatley's work—including her choice of subject matter—depended upon white approval and publication practice. It is clear that early African American literature, though critical to the African American liberation movement, could not engage in overt cultural critique of the riot scene, especially given the ways in which the systems supporting white privilege tended to catch black dissidents in a political, social, and very violent web of circumstances.

The rich oral tradition of African American culture also existed before the black press; however, it was also a targeted medium of expression. African American orature incites social changes; however, when it reaches beyond the confines of the black community, it is targeted because of the threat it poses to white supremacy. For instance, although black women's orature is a powerful means of social commentary, the position of women in apartheid cultures tends to silence their subversions outside of the public view. Sojourner Truth's demise as an orator of black women's experience was tellingly silenced in her articulation of the nineteenth-century call for women's rights. Her twentieth-century counterparts, as Angela Davis might testify, were also challenged by a hegemony that sought to discredit their messages by recasting their activism as gendered rather than racial responses. The voices of black women have also been silenced by calls for their sexual and social subjugation to the black men that they are literally accused of loving. As such, Davis's detention based on charges that she conspired with her lover to assassinate a public official made her vulnerable to this kind of sexualized silencing. The apartheid state is also unerringly exact in its persecution of black male orators. As Michael Eric Dyson points out, the unusually parallel deaths of Martin Luther King, Jr., Malcolm X, Tupac Shakur, and — because he embodied the threat of black male excess in his valorization of black urban culture — Christopher "Biggie Smalls" Wallace each suggest that when black male voices publicly engage white supremacy, death is the ultimate mechanism of silence.[22]

It is my sense, then, that it is doubly important to focus on the black press and African American fiction as the ultimate witnesses to white riot. Black presses existed prior to the emergence of the black novel as a medium of cultural and social protest. The black press originated in 1827 with the founding of the first black newspaper, *Freedom's Journal,* by Samuel Cornish and John B. Russwurm. Frederick Douglass's *North Star,* first published in 1841, predated the first novel published by an African American, Harriet E. Wilson's *Our Nig,* by eighteen years.[23] These two media rewrite the depiction of riot in both historical and literary narratives.

Although the black press can be documented as a means of resistance to white domination, the historical record shows that the press is subject to the effects of racialized ululation. The black press, as the saga of the *Wilmington Daily Record* indicates, is subject to destruction, usually by fire, at the hands of those who would denounce any threat to the veracity of the discourse of white privilege. The office that housed Alexander L. Manly's *Record* was burned in 1898 because Manly questioned the record of his race that was preserved in the majority annals. Other black presses of the era were also deliberately destroyed. Ida B. Wells-Barnett's newspaper, *Free Speech,* was similarly silenced in 1892 when she printed an editorial about a lynching inspired by a race rape in Memphis.[24] The burning of the *Record* and other black presses by the white citizenry is linguistically and culturally symbolic of the attempt to destroy the historical record of white riot.[25]

These facts speak to the incendiary nature of the black press. Most black presses have been tried by fire, whether as a result of arson or the lack of governmental protection (the black firemen of Wilmington were detained by members of the militia until it seemed that the *Record* fire might spread to neighboring buildings) because they threaten to incite social change. The relationship between the black press and periods of social upheaval is evident in the sense that numerous black presses owe their existence to periods marked by racialized ululation and the violence that arose from such agitation.

Racialized violence that was described as "race riots" broke out in the South, North, and West from 1866 to 1923.[26] In response to this, or more precisely, part of the call for and response to this, was the establishment of black newspapers during this time. The *California Voice*,[27] *Call-Missouri*,[28] *Chicago Whip*, and *Negro World*[29] all grew out of the unrest of the 1900s. Each paper was launched in 1919, a pivotal moment in American riot history. One should also note that the publication of the *Houston Observer* (1916–1931) coincided with the Houston race riot of 1917. Further, the *Oklahoma Eagle*, started in 1922, was published the first year after the Tulsa riots of 1921. The black press, then, becomes identified with the protest tradition; it is a part of the reaction to the white racialized ululation of the period. However, due to the black press's particular history of destruction by fire, African American fiction, most particularly historical fiction, is the medium that resists the invisibility of white riot.

In South Africa, the unmasking of white riot is also difficult. In order to understand the ways in which this masking works in South Africa, I begin this examination at the place where, interestingly, most non-black South Africans begin when they examine the cultural milieu of South Africa: with the colonization and occupation of the land. I do not begin at this historical point in order to legitimize the mythology of white land rights in the regions; I begin here because the origins of white riot in South Africa lie in the origins of Afrikaner consciousness. After Jan van Riebeeck established an outpost on the Cape of Good Hope in 1652, the ethnically based violence ruptured existing social structures in the region. When the Dutch arrived they violated the San/Koi-Khoin,[30] both literally—through the taking of sexual partners in a social setting that requires a recognition of an extended clan relationship—and linguistically—through the naming and claiming of both their land and their identities.[31] The legacy continues in the identity struggles of the South African "races." There are still distinctions between the black South Africans, Afrikaners, coloureds, and the Cape coloureds, the progeny of Dutch and San/Koi-Khoin intermingling.[32]

During the apartheid era the government defined racial identity in order to displace black South Africans. Through such linguistic bastardization, Xhosas became "kaffirs," due to the inability of the Afrikaner tongue to reproduce the clicks that characterize the Xhosa language, one of the legacies of its San linguistic heritage. And this misnaming occurred in the midst of white expansionism into the hinterland from 1652 when the land, a part of the cultural identity of the black ethnic groups of the region, was also renamed as a nation. These linguistic slippages continued after 1948 when apartheid became codified in this new nation. While Afrikaner identity was being constructed in the 1950s, the South African government used figurative language to repatriate the black South African. As such, the term *bantu* replaced *native* in the official discourse, and black South African identity was dismantled with the passage of the Bantu Authorities Act in 1951. Thus, *bantu*—a word that once denoted humanness—was robbed of its original meaning and made offensive through this official appropriation.[33] What begins as linguistic displacement culminates in a history that is marked by the practice and language of legal repression. This displacement is of particular relevance when looking at the act of white riot and how it is represented in the apartheid-era South African press.

The history of legal repression in South Africa is particularly focused on limiting press freedoms. Not only do the restrictions affect press coverage but they inevitably make the establishment of a true black press impossible. Under the Suppression of Communism Act, No. 44 of 1950 (amended by Act 76 of 1962 and Act 97 of 1965):

No new newspaper may be registered unless the proprietor deposits with the Minister of the Interior such amount, not exceeding R20,000, as the Minister may determine, or unless the Minister certifies that he has no reason to believe that it will at any time be necessary for him to prohibit the paper.[34]

At least five additional acts passed into law by the South African government limited press freedoms in the country, effectively controlling the licensing of presses and providing a legal base for the censure of individual members of the press.[35] Apartheid law insisted that newspapers, film, and other written documents "take cognizance of the complex racial problems of South Africa, the general good and the safety of the country and its peoples."[36] Although staffed by black editors and writers, the newspapers that served the majority black community prior to the repeal of the apart-

heid laws were all owned by white publishers.[37] However, due to the censorship laws these presses could not always effectively document antiapartheid struggle, including the racialized violence that has been associated
with it.

How, then, is it possible to document the existence of white riot? The
literature of protest in America and South Africa revises the historical record of racial oppression and the violence associated with it; the texts me-
diate the misrepresented histories of these communities, especially when
the social fabric is contextualized by riot, both the white and the raced.
And given the history of separation based on race and ethnicity in the culture, these texts must inevitably address the politics of citizenship in the
United States and South Africa. The specific intersection of race and riot
in societies that are clearly racialized is what unites Wilmington, Soweto,
Los Angeles, and Mmabatho. Each proceeds along the same course: from
white racialized ululation, to white riot, finally proceeding to a focus on
race riot, a process that ignores the existence of the first two stages. The
deliberate misrepresentation of white riot in American and South African
cultures certainly fits into Hayden White's assertion that the difference between historical representations is made possible by the fact that historiog-
raphy is a nonscientific field. White makes the difference between contest-
ing histories palatable by making room for the "historical imagination." [38]
However, the historical imaginations in the United States and South Africa
are based on palates amenable to the tastes of white supremacy. Thus the
notion of white supremacy at work in these nations makes white riot difficult to locate. In this exploration of the apartheid imagination of racial
violence, I focus on the ways in which the racialized society imagines itself
at moments when the collision of race and culture culminate in a riot event.
However, the chapters that follow unmask the white riots at the center of
these episodes of racial violence by documenting the literary, journalistic,
narrative, and film histories of these events.

Reading the Riot Act

The Teleology of Charles Chesnutt's *The Marrow*
of Tradition and the Wilmington Race Riot of 1898

I was at the ironing table, when one of my little ones ran in and told me
that the school house was on fire. I hurried out to join the crowd of
anxious mothers . . . but we were not able to get past the crowd of men
who surrounded the *Record* building. The cries of the frightened children
could be heard, and the inability of the mothers to reach them added to the
horror of the scene. . . . One little girl died of sheer fright. The shooting
without, mingled with the oaths of the men and the frantic wails of the
women within, were too much for the little one to bear.
　　　　　　　　　　　　　　　　　　　　　　　—Adelaide Peterson, 1899

[G]o to the polls tomorrow and if you find the Negro out voting, tell him
to leave the polls and if he refuses, kill him, shoot him down in his tracks.
　　　　　　　　　　　　　　　　　　　　　　—Alfred Moore Waddell, 1898

On the morning of November 10th, when the party of men led by Colonel
A. M. Waddell, destroyed the newspaper plant, the riot . . . started.
　　　　　　　　　　　　　　　　　　　　　　　—Thomas W. Clawson, n.d.

It was claimed among the political campaigners that in the eastern portion
of North Carolina, the white people were under Negro rule. They took
advantage of this scarecrow, and held it up before the white friends of the
Negro in all their political speeches, using also the Manly article to create
anger among the loyal and conservative white citizens.
　　　　　　　　　　　　　　　　　　　　　　　—Rev. J. Allen Kirk, 1898

I n her witness narrative of the race riot in Wilmington, North Carolina,
in 1898, Adelaide Peterson provides us with a provocative remembrance
of the scene. Included in Jack Thorne's novel, *Hanover; or, The Persecu-*

tion of the Lowly, the narrative was one of many witness statements David Bryant Fulton collected for his novel about the incident which he published under the Thorne pseudonym. Peterson ends her narrative by texturizing the racial and sexual undercurrents of the violence. Note her description of the following scene:

I will not close this narrative without mentioning an act of bravery performed by a lone woman which stopped the vulgar and inhuman searching of women in our section of the city. The most atrocious and unpardonable act of the mob was the wanton disregard for womanhood. Lizzie Smith was the first woman to make a firm and stubborn stand against the proceeding in the southern section. It was near the noon hour when Lizzie, homeward bound, reached the corner of Orange and Third Street. A block away she saw a woman struggling to free herself from the grasp of several men who were, in turn, slapping her face and otherwise abusing her. The woman fought until her clothes were torn to shreds; then with a shove the men allowed her to proceed on her way. Lizzie could have saved herself by running away, but anger at such cowardice had chased away every vestige of her fear. She leisurely walked up to where the fight was going on. "Halt," said one of the ruffians to Lizzie, "an' let's see how many razors you got under them duds. That tother wench was er walkin' arsennel. Come now!" roared the man, "none er your cussed impert'nence." Lizzie, instead of assaying to comply, akimbowed and looked defiantly at the crowd about her. "Oh, yo' po' white trash."

"Shut up or we'll set you an' have done with it," said the leader, making a motion toward his hip pocket. "Yo' will, eh!" answered the girl, "yo' kan't skeer me. But ef yo' wanter search me I'll take off ma clothes, so yo' won't have ter tear 'em," and Lizzie began to hurriedly unfasten her bodice. "You've got ter search me right," she continued, throwing off piece after piece; "yo'll fin' I am jes' like yo' sisters an' mamies, yo' po' tackies." "That'll do," growled one of the men, as Lizzie was unbuttoning the last piece. "Oh, no," returned the girl, "I'm goin ter git naked; yer got ter see that I'm er woman." White women were looking on from their windows at this sight so shocking. One had the courage to shout "Shame! How dare you expose that woman in that manner?" "Them's the curnel's orders," replied the leader, raising his hat. "Who is the Colonel, and what right has he to give such orders?" shrieked the woman. "You ought to be ashamed of yourselves for your own wives and daughters' sakes." The men skulked away and left Lizzie victor on the field.[1]

This incident reveals the ways the social and cultural mindset of the community exacerbates the riot situation by focusing on representative bodies, bodies that symbolize the racial constructions of a particular space and time. In Peterson's narrative, it is clear that the black female body lies at the center of the racialized violence. The black female body becomes defined both through white male sexual oppression and through white female voyeurism. This image of the black female body is one that is made available for violation, juxtaposed against the communal definition of pure white womanhood. Peterson's narrative describes the place of the black woman in the riot space; she is both victim and survivor, participant and witness. The unnamed woman is the victim of the white rioters in their process of following the "curnel's orders," their license mirroring the impunity of the white rapists that A. L. Manly accuses in his editorial about race rape in the South.

It is apparent that the nakedness of the unnamed woman arouses the white male rioters. Quite simply—though I am, perhaps, stating the obvious—they view Lizzie Smith through the peculiar sexual license that the practice of white supremacy grants white males. Smith's body is susceptible to being stripped naked by virtue of her gender and her race; in this space determined by the racial and gender legacies of the Confederacy, hers is the body most available to white domination. In the midst of the riot space, she is the pornographic embodied. Without the necessity of her consent or willingness to participate, Smith fails to provide the erotic racial encounter her antagonists expected principally because there is another level of arousal that influences this scene. What, for instance, can be inferred from the silence of the white female witnesses who must have also seen the nakedness of Lizzie Smith's predecessor? As Peterson's text reveals they are participants in her oppression, sharing in the pleasure of the scene. Tellingly, they refuse to break their silence *before* Smith begins to signify on the white rioters. From their position of privilege on the pedestal of white supremacy, they intervene only after Smith's signifying threatens to disrupt white male authority. The relationship between race and gender that this incident makes evident is crucial to our understanding of the experience of white riot. Indisputably, the Peterson narrative places whites in the midst of the riot space as the active rather than the reactive participants. With its focus on white riot the narrative describes the collision of race and culture in the Wilmington race riot of 1898. Interestingly, it also describes the racial and sexual dynamics at work in numerous episodes of violence at the turn of the twentieth century. The events that led to the racialized violence in 1898, those that preceded it, and those that follow are intimately connected. The connection is maintained in race-based cultural systems that thrive on adversarial relationships between blacks and whites, turning on the ways in which black bodies are structured in the midst of racial violence.

There are, in fact, representative bodies at the center of every riot event. In the United States, class- and race-based violence typically centers on media-generated images of the black male. The videotaped beating of Rodney King, which aired worldwide almost daily after the incident occurred in March 1992, is only one example of how the media constructs the black male body as both a symbol of and an invitation to aggression.[2] Almost a

century earlier the press also witnesses the November 1898 riot in Wilmington, North Carolina, where the black male body was the focus of white
racialized ululation. Historical documents, attesting to the near hysteria
generated in the majority press where the black press is concerned, point to
an editorial published in the *Wilmington Daily Record,* one of the few black-
owned daily newspapers in the country, as the precursor of the unrest.[3] On
18 August 1898, Alexander Lightfoot Manly, the African American editor
of the paper, responded to a speech given by Rebecca Felton, a white "femi-
nist" who was invested in the politics of southern white womanhood. While
speaking at an agricultural meeting in Georgia, Felton advocated lynching
black men whom she characterized as habitually roaming the countryside
to rape white women.[4] According to Felton, "if it needs lynching to protect
woman's dearest possession from the ravening human beasts—then I say
lynch, a thousand times a week, if necessary."[5] In an attempt to call attention to the number of black women raped by white men who assaulted them
without fear of legal repercussion, Manly responded to Felton insisting that
society should punish rape regardless of the race of the rapist. Manly's
assertion that white race rapes were widespread, though quite accurate,
was immediately denied by the white community through the conservative
presses that served Wilmington's white gentry and masses.[6]

Outraged white newspaper editors protested that the remarks were in-
sulting to white womanhood and instigated a riot, one that was fought by
lower-class whites and led by Wilmington's white aristocracy. Inciting their
readership, they essentially waged a war against the state's black population. It was a war that waited, however, for the appropriate moment to
escalate; coinciding with the November elections, the "race riot" began
three months later. And it erupted in the midst of racialized ululation origi-
nating in the press. The message of the 7 November 1898 masthead of
the *Wilmington Evening Dispatch*—"Let Every Anglo-Saxon Remember the
Duty He Owes to His Race"—is indicative of this manipulation. It was a
call to arms, a precursor to the white riot in Wilmington.

At the risk of being inciteful, I include a portion of the Manly editorial,
"Mrs. Felton's Speech":

This woman makes a strong plea for womanhood, and if the alleged crimes of
rape were half so frequent as oftimes reported, her plea would be worthy of con-
sideration.

Mrs. Felton, like many other so-called Christians, loses sight of the basic principle of the religion of Christ in her plea for one class of people as against another.
. . . The morals of the poor white people are on par with their colored neighbors

of like conditions, and if any one doubts the statement let him visit among them. The whole lump needs to be leavened by those who profess so much religion and showing them that the preservation of virtue is an essential for the life of any people.

Mrs. Felton begins well for she admits that education will better protect the girls on the farm from the assaulter. This we admit and it should not be confined to the white any more than to the colored girls. The papers are filled often with reports of rapes of white women, and the subsequent lynching of the alleged rapists. The editors pour forth volleys of aspersions against all negroes because of the few who may be guilty. If the papers and speakers of the other race would condemn the commission of crime because it is crime and not try to make it appear that the negroes were the only criminals, they would find their strongest allies in the intelligent negroes themselves, and together the whites and blacks would root the evil out of both races.

We suggest that the whites guard their women more closely, as Mrs. Felton says, thus giving no opportunity for the human fiend, be he white or black. You leave your goods out of doors and then complain because they are taken away.

Poor white men are careless in the matter of protecting their women, especially on farms. They are careless of their conduct toward them, and our experience among poor white people in the country teaches us that the women of that race are not any more particular in the matter of clandestine meetings with colored men, than are white men with colored women. Meetings of this kind go on for some time until the woman's infatuation or the man's boldness bring attention to them and the man is lynched for rape. Every negro lynched is called a "big burly, black brute," when in fact many of those who have thus been dealt with had white men for their fathers, and were not only not "black" and "burly" but were sufficiently attractive for white girls of culture and refinement to fall in love with them as is well known to all.

Mrs. Felton must begin at the fountain head if she wishes to purify the stream.

Teach your men purity. Let virtue be something more than an excuse for them to intimidate and torture a helpless people. Tell your men that it is no worse for a black man to be intimate with a white woman, than for a white man to be intimate with a colored woman.

You set yourselves down as a lot of carping hypocrites; in fact you cry aloud for the virtue of your women while you seek to destroy the morality of ours. Don't think ever that your women will remain pure white while you are debauching ours. You sow the seed—the harvest will come in due time.[7]

Wilmington's white editors and politicians—indeed editors across North Carolina—reprinted the article to support a campaign of white supremacy. Excerpts of it were included in public speeches, and used—in and out of context—in newspapers and in anonymously published political broadsides. The editorials accompanying the reprints became the wellspring of the racialized ululation that culminated in the "Wilmington Race Riot." It might seem that the content of the editorial was so incendiary, so novel, or so provocative that it generated racial violence spontaneously. However, it was neither the first nor the most provocative of such editorials published in the black press specifically centered on "race rape" and the discourse on gender and on race and class miscegenation. Ida B. Wells-Barnett published similar pieces as early as 1892 in the form of newspaper articles, pamphlets, and protest texts.[8] Given the white reaction to the Manly editorial, it is clear that its use in the white press and in political broadsides was calculated to provoke white riot.

Manly's editorial was objectionable to the "Democratic" agenda not because it was false, but because he attacked white supremacist notions of religion, class and race stereotypes, and morality. Manly pointed to the lack of Christian ethics that Felton's call for lynching reveals. Succinctly, Manly publicly questioned the very underpinnings of the divine southern right of white rule. Manly further contravened white supremacist ideology in his discussion of interracial relationships. Not only did he question the racial and sexual boundaries of white supremacy, he also questioned the notion of white female sexual purity in his assertion that they desired sexual liaisons with black men, indeed, that they could express any sexual desire at all. By discussing the racial and sexual boundaries established in Wilmington of 1898, Manly was attempting to remove the black male body from the center of the racialized ululation.

Manly also articulated the possibility that class-based similarities between the races existed. Southern white political power had long been maintained by erasing all notions of difference between whites. White social unity was based on race difference, on the necessity to maintain racial purity. Manly's focus on class rather than race threatened the core of the race-based political allegiance in the state. The white aristocracy labored to bridge class boundaries in order to promote white unity prior to the riot. One attempt to create the illusion of a classless white society appeared as "Ignorance and Poverty" in an 1898 broadside denouncing Negro rule. Ascribed to a poor white member of the Democratic Party—aptly dubbed Musselwhite in keeping with white supremacist propaganda—the authors foreground race rather than class in their response to the Manly editorial:

The honest people of Robeson county are tired of the present disgraceful administration, and *I* believe all white men who love and honor their country and State, who revere law and good government, who oppose the blight of negro domination, who favor white supremacy will and should come together and vote as brothers. *We* believe that all white men who love and honor their country and State, who revere the law and good government, who oppose the blight of negro domination, who favor white supremacy will and should come together and vote as brothers. We are quoted as being "petted" by Democrats which is untrue. It requires neither riches, knowledge, coaxing nor persuasion to learn white from black.[9]

Obviously, the Musselwhite article attempts to counter Manly's point that class, rather than race, determines social mores. Perhaps more problematically for the southern white power structure, Manly had insisted that a racially just solution effected by both races was necessary and possible. In his editorial he argues that the difference between black and white *was learned*. In so doing his editorial attacked the prevailing notions of white social supremacy. The crux of his editorial, then, threatened to make white-defined race and class distinctions tenuous. Manly's accusations—especially his discussion of white men and women voluntarily participating in miscegenation coupled with his insistence upon black social, cultural, and moral agency—tenaciously denied their plausibility.

In concert with the black feminists of his era, Manly addresses the devaluation of the bodies of women of color in a white supremacist society that are implicit in Felton's remarks.[10] Predictably, a majority of the responses to Manly's editorial were aimed at his slander of white women, a slander that took on both political and sexual overtones. In response to the moral upbraiding Manly presented in the editorial, the writers of the broadsides equated race rape with Republican rule. The political agenda of the white ruling class of Wilmington was to maintain Democratic rule, thereby retaining the privileges of white supremacy. The riot was a necessary component of this political agenda.

At least two separate Democratic conspiracies precipitated the "riot" of 10 November 1898.[11] At the risk of belaboring my point, I should delimit how the racialized violence of Wilmington 1898 is defined from the dual perspectives of race which white supremacy makes necessary. In essence, black and white riot survivors seem to have experienced two very different events. Documentation of the event in the minority press, memoirs, and narratives refer to the incident as the "Wilmington Massacre of 1898." Accounts published in the white press of the period describe the incident as the "Wilmington Race Riot of 1898." The differing nomenclatures call attention to a dissonance between the two races that goes well beyond matters of journalistic slant. It was certainly a massacre; a Gatling gun fired at unarmed people can be nothing less. However, as the textual evidence shows, majority custom colorizes the violence by naming it a "race riot" and inserting rioting black bodies in the midst of the riot scene.

How do these terms, *massacre* and *riot,* limn the disparity between how the different segments of the society historicize the event? Obviously, the way a history is documented relates to the relationship between cultural stasis and cultural disruption, between riot and renewal. My emphasis is on the teleology of these designations that describe a history of a massacre in which African Americans were killed by *rioting whites* who were fighting against the phantom of "negro rule." Yet histories recorded within the reflexive glare of white supremacy define race riot by displacing both the cause and source of the violence.[12] In order to make the white rioters visible it is necessary to insist upon a more definitive description of their actions than our current understanding of the term *race riot* allows. Operating under the delusion of "negro rule" that was proliferated in preelection press accounts, white rioters sought to reinscribe their political and social power in Wilmington.

Although weapons were not readily available to the black community, there was armed resistance from it. However, there is evidence of only one white fatality during the riot.[13] Where, then, is the evidence of the rioting black bodies that are supposed to have dominated the riot scene? Instead, the persistence of a black middle class in the Wilmington of 1898 and today—indeed, the presence of the *Wilmington Journal,* built near the same sight as the *Record*—bears witness to the fact that African Americans, at least partially, reclaimed their social place after the riot. Despite the white racialized ululation and the violence that ensued, black communities did survive Wilmington's riot. Indeed, it is the persistency of black belongingness that always eventually drives the hegemony into a frenzy of racialized ululation utilizing the language of white supremacy to birth the notion of white riots.

Politicians and pressmen who were proponents of white supremacy used the language of miscegenation to incite white riot in Wilmington, 1898. It is a language that Chesnutt reinscribes in his fictional rendering of the riot in *The Marrow of Tradition.* His fictionalization of the white riot ultimately preserves the historical experience as a white riot, a move that allowed him to write unaffected by the "ideals" of white supremacy. Although the white press describes the riot as a spontaneous reaction to the Manly editorial, the violence actually erupted three months later on the day following the November elections. In the months that followed the publication of this editorial, the majority presses of Wilmington created a state of race and class panic in the white population of Wilmington. It is important to examine the teleology of the white riot in Wilmington in order to read Charles Chesnutt's *The Marrow of Tradition* as a revisionist history of the event.

THE POLITICS OF RACE: THE TELEOLOGICAL TRACE OF WILMINGTON'S WHITE RIOT

The racialized ululation that began early in the decade is the prelude to Wilmington's white riot. At the turn of the century, numerous papers including the *Caucasian,* whose very name conjures notions of hierarchy based on racial difference, served the causes of white supremacy in North Carolina. Josephus Daniels, the North Carolinian who created the media campaign designed to control the growth of black political power, advocated the use of lower-class whites to enforce the dominant social structure.[14] As editor of the *Raleigh Times* and writer for several other white presses, Daniels's influence can be measured by the number of presses that replicated his editorial policies throughout the South and the number of presses influenced by his editorial policies in the North.

Let me emphasize that Daniels's ideological stance and, indeed, the manner in which the press disseminated it were not limited to the South. In fact, Alexander Manly read Felton's remarks in the *New York Times.* The *Times* covered the aftermath of the events in Wilmington and similar racial incidents in South Carolina, what it referenced as the "race wars" on 17 and 18 November. Both issues seemingly reported events protesting the "race wars," although nothing is reported of how the southern white press initiated the unrest. In the same issues, however, the *Times,* like its southern counterparts, represented black males as a force needing to be controlled in these events. White supremacy, it seems, had its place on both sides of the Mason-Dixon line.

It is clear that racist ideology defined both the North and the South in 1898. It is impossible to take seriously the notion that the North had a different orientation to racism than the South in 1898 since the practice of racism negates the imaginary cultural divide. A 17 November 1898 *Times* article entitled "Two More Fights at Pana" provides a telling example of this kind of cultural contiguity between the North and the South. The article describes a fatal encounter between a striking white male miner and an African American man who was used as a strike-breaker during the 1898 strike in Illinois. White mine workers were typical examples of the lower-class whites who were pitted against blacks in the politics of racialized division:

The first battle was started by an unruly negro firing upon Wesley Pope, . . . conversing with his wife . . . Pope was unarmed, but went in his home and secured a Winchester . . . he fired upon the negro, and was soon joined by other strikers, the negro after falling twice beneath the din of bullets, was driven into an adjacent cornfield where he sought shelter. B [*sic*] of Bloomington turned out immediately with a Gatling gun, and the firing restarted. . . .

Over 500 shots were exchanged but the effect could not be ascertained.[15] (emphasis mine)

Able to work in the midst of the strike, able to absorb hundreds of shots from an array of increasingly deadly weapons, the "unruly negro" assumes a virility of superhuman proportions. Like Melville's Babo in "Benito Cereno," he symbolizes a power which his white attackers are compelled to control yet cannot. The journalistic style of the article linguistically marks "the negro" as an uncontrollable agent, one that by reason of his race is at once their socioeconomic inferior as he breaks the strike lines and their genetic superior as he withstands an assault of five hundred shots. As I shall discuss in the succeeding chapters, this reaction to the physical supremacy of blackness defines white racial violence. The white characters in the text are mere respondents whose actions are reported figuratively in the passive voice. While the "negro," linguistically marked as an aggressor, fires on an unarmed man, the Gatling gun—not "B of Bloomington," who is linguistically marked by the agentless passive—restarts the firing. The responsibility of the white participants is thus erased. The agentless passive negates any admission of white aggression in this exchange. It is also clear that this kind of linguistic displacement produces a suspension of reality that explains why the five-hundred-shot volley had no ascertainable effect on Pope's black body.[16]

White "Democratic" accounts of the incident also use this linguistic construction to displace responsibility for the events in Wilmington. Andrew Howell's account of the beginning of the riot—which he dedicates, in part, to Colonel Alfred M. Waddell, one of the leaders of Wilmington's white riot—reveals this linguistic displacement:

A number of men broke into the printing office for the purpose of throwing out the outfit that published the paper. The equipment was thrown into the street. Then *it was discovered that the building was on fire in the second story. It was thought that an overturned lamp had caused the blaze.* . . .

Later in the morning . . . one of the black men drew a pistol and deliberately shot at a group of white men standing not far away. *There was a return fire from Winchester rifles and pistols.* Several colored [*sic*] men fell. . . .

There were other unfortunate casualties among the negroes, due to indiscreet acts and refusal to submit to the inevitable.[17] (emphasis mine)

Again the agentless passive displaces white aggression while naming the black man as an agent in his own "inevitable" destruction. Other majority-authored texts about Wilmington of the 1890s ignored white racialized violence, leaving a telling absence in the histories.[18]

The use of passive linguistic constructions not only shifts the emphasis away from white racial violence, it also portrays the black male as extrahuman, simultaneously alien and familiar, both physically superior and culturally inferior. I am suggesting that these portrayals reveal a dual characterization of the black male body: it is devoid of power, yet imbued with an alien-like physical tenacity. The block-type headlines prefigure a "black type" always connected with violence. These are the kinds of media-driven stereotypes that Manly attempts to debunk in the 18 August editorial. The white supremacist response disseminated through the press and political broadsides reinforces the stereotype of the "burly black male" and white hysteria over the power of Negro rule through the use of sensationalized block headlines, mastheads, and typefaces. Tellingly, a single Democratic broadside includes the following phrases in block type: "BEARING ITS FRUIT: The Slanderous Article of the Wilmington Negro Paper; A RACE RIOT IMMINENT," "NEGRO RULE IN CRAVEN COUNTY," "NEGRO MOBS STAND BY THE EDITOR," and "DEFAMER OF WHITE WOMEN—HISTORY REPEATS ITSELF."[19] This kind of racialized ululation in the press is represented by the 8 November 1898 edition of the *Wilmington Daily Messenger*, which proclaims, "Lawless Negroes," "Negroes Intend to Control," and "Whites Determined to Throw Off Negro Rule . . . ."

This call to arms is also suggested by the deceptively innocent headline, "Guns Still Coming to N.C." The article is actually a harbinger of the white violence because it informs readers of the increase in firearms pouring into Wilmington.[20] The message is that racial violence, facilitated by the sale of firearms to whites, is imminent. Racial and sexual tension, deliberately reconstructed with media black types/block types become the means through which affluent whites retain power not only over blacks but also over the poor whites who found after the riot that white unity, like the Negro rule they had rioted against, was nonexistent.[21] Through the power of racialized discourse, the white press of the time, then, unites white society across class lines on the question of how power relationships determine the slope of the "color line."

White power agitation by the press, using agent-active descriptions for African American violent responses and agentless-passive descriptions for the white racialized violence to which they respond, characterizes the violence in 1898 Wilmington. As the white hysteria reached a crescendo, Thomas Clawson, the editor of the *Wilmington Daily Messenger*, responded to Manly's editorial by demanding an immediate retraction, not just from

Manly, but also from the black community as a whole. Clawson's *Messenger* remained at the center of the racialized ululation. It was through the *Messenger,* in fact, that Alfred Moore Waddell summoned some of Wilmington's most prominent African American citizens, including Manly's father-in-law, Frederick Sadgwar, and Dr. Thomas R. Mask, who would later play an important role in the riot and in Chesnutt's portrayal of it in *The Marrow of Tradition.* Waddell, an attorney by training and former Confederate colonel, was conspicuously unemployed at the time he assumed a leadership role for the Democratic political machinations.[22] The summoned representatives of the African American community were given a list of demands that called for a retraction of Manly's article and an order that Manly and his brothers leave Wilmington. Interestingly, their urgency was largely symbolic. Masquerading as white, Manly had already left Wilmington and many of the white agitators, including Clawson, were aware of this fact.

While the *Record* was the only daily black press in the area, Wilmington also had several newspapers that served the white community at the time of the riot.[23] Wilmington readers had access to morning and evening papers in addition to other less frequently published papers. The *Messenger* (founded in May 1887) and the *Dispatch* (founded in 1867 and touted as a "champion of conservative politics"),[24] then, became the means through which racial tension was created. Their reportage reveals the root problem: the fear of "rule by men of African origin." In their attempt to control the responses of the white community, the writers of the *Messenger* and *Dispatch* advocated purging Wilmington of the middle-class blacks. Political power in the black community lay with the black middle class, which was composed of members of the clergy, the black press, and entrepreneurs. The majority press targeted these particular segments of black society, leaving the more impoverished members of both races to succumb to the control of the upper-class white majority.

While the black underclass in the United States has always been visible, impoverished whites were rendered invisible by white supremacist notions of whiteness that is classless, at least in the public sphere. Who, then, comprised the white underclass in Wilmington at the turn of the century?[25] In addition to poor southern whites, Wilmington had a large Irish and Scottish immigrant population. Having established themselves early in the nineteenth century, Scottish immigrants reported both professional and service occupations by the 1850 census. The Irish, conversely, did not report the same degree of assimilation, due in part to a history of immigration that both identified them with and separated them from African Americans.

More than two million Irish entered the United States between 1845 and 1855.[26] Half of those who attempted the voyage, many of whom embarked on ships that had been christened in the Trans-Atlantic Slave Trade, died in their own version of the Middle Passage. Wilmington's 1850 census revealed a substantial block of employed Irish immigrants settled in the city; however, by the 1890s, the last wave of Irish immigrants, like their non-immigrant poor white counterparts, lived in substandard conditions and were largely unemployed. The Irish early became a moving force in forming labor unions in the North;[27] however, in the nonunionized South, as Wilmington demonstrates, Irish "union" affiliation was with the Redshirts, the precursor to the Ku Klux Klan. The employment of whites became one of the primary focuses of the racialized ululation preceding the riot. The racialized ululation preceding the riot blamed white poverty and unemployment on black workers. So, for Irish immigrants in Wilmington, attaining whiteness—the process of replacing an ethnic identity for a racial identity—was integral to their participation in the white riot. Essentially, the Irish embraced white supremacy in order to make their whiteness visible.[28]

In addition to constructing their racialized ululation around issues of class and race, the white press gendered the discourse surrounding the riot. These editorials were effective because the authors manipulated the traditional symbol of white womanhood in southern patriarchal social structure. Let me return to the *Times* coverage of the Pana incident to examine the ways in which this practice makes the notion of gender integral to the white supremacist movement. Note that the violence took place in the presence of Wesley Pope's unnamed wife. Her presence defines the incendiary and *inciteful* moment that "justifies" the white violence in this instance. In the Wilmington debate the editors of the majority press couched their dialogue in terms of protecting the purity of white womanhood, while Manly's editorial focused on the sexual victimization of black women. As these examples reveal, control of the female body symbolizes male power and remains at the center of the riot event.

It is important to have some sense of what this dominion over female space signifies and/or silences. Integral to Manly's position is the fact that the Wilmington uprising occurred in a period during which black men were routinely lynched for "assaulting" white women. It did not matter whether the assault involved actual physical contact or whether the sexual contact was initiated with the consent of both parties. In fact, so many African American men died by lynching during this period that conservative estimates indicate the number to be over 150 each year from 1880 through 1890. Indeed, over 230 men died in 1892, a fact in keeping with my open-

ing comments about the preoccupation with cultural violence at the turn
of the century.[29] Surely Alexander Manly wrote his editorial at a precarious time both for the black press and anti–white supremacist discourse;
despite this context he continually used his press to attack white privilege
with significant results.[30]

In order to explore the cultural importance of Manly and, later, the
compelling reasons why Chesnutt fictionalizes him in *Marrow,* it is necessary to examine Manly's place in 1898 Wilmington. Born 13 May 1866 near
Raleigh, North Carolina, Alexander Lightfoot Manly—described as a voluntary black due to his white appearance—brought a provocative genealogy to the riot scene. Manly's paternal grandfather was Charles Manly,
who was governor of North Carolina from 1849 to 1851.[31] Acknowledging his parental responsibility to his enslaved children, Governor Manly
manumitted them and provided them with land and farm equipment. Due
to this the Manlys had achieved some measure of middle-class status early
in the century. Manly attended Hampton Institute where he was trained as
a painter.[32] Manly's wife, Carrie Sadgwar, was a member of Wilmington's
black high society, belonging to a family with a provocative genealogy of
its own.[33] Manly's involvement in the community and his willingness to
engage in discussions about African American issues relates to the radical agency of the early black press, given his quest to correct the image of
African Americans in the media. This is particularly evident in his editorial
regarding his concern for the newsprint type-casting of the "burly, black
brute."

The black types perpetuated in the headlines of the era and subsequent
documents about the riot used distorted versions of Manly's editorial that
highlighted Manly's disrespect for white women and his focus on the social
activities of "poor whites." Although only two copies of the *Record* are extant, the price of the paper reveals its popularity. At a time when the *New
York Times* sold for one cent in New York, two cents elsewhere, the price
of the *Record* had increased from ten cents per month to twenty-five cents
per month by November 1898. The price exceeded that of both majority
presses, and given the majority African American population in Wilmington and the high literacy rates of this group, the circulation is estimated to
have been significant, although no exact figures are available. The masthead
of the *Record* evokes the extent of its subscribership stating simply that
the circulation is "large." That the paper was well read by white Wilming-
tonians is certain as a cursory glance at its advertisements reveals; this also
highlights white Wilmington's preoccupation with blackness.

Yet such typecasting does not begin to characterize the peculiar inter-

Alexander L. Manly, editor of the *Wilmington Daily Record* (Photograph by Lielman; courtesy of Cape Fear Museum, Wilmington, N.C., no. 986.26.5, Manly Collection)

action of race and political ideology at work in Wilmington. Even the *How* press that Manly purchased to print the *Record* is indicative of this interaction. Ironically, Manly and his brothers established the *Record* about 1887 after purchasing a used press from Thomas Clawson, the white supremacist editor of the *Messenger*. Clawson had purchased the press from John C. Abbott, whom he described as "a Carpet-bagger politician from the North [who] . . . had joined some other Wilmington Republican scalawags in the publication of a daily."[34] The power of the How press, like the myth of classless whiteness, could suit the conveniences of the political moment. Manly continued to publish the paper after he refused to print a retraction of his editorial; this decision, however, was not without consequences. After being forced out of his lease, he moved the press from the main business area to Wilmington's black business district on Seventh Street.[35] However, the discourse of white racialized ululation made it clear that the destruction of his press was imminent. Supported by the black community, Manly published until late October when violence was described in the white press as being "inevitable."[36] During this period of time the *Record,* by its very existence, seemed to have been the subject of an on-going dialogue with the white press, a dialogue that ignited the white community and precipitated the violence. The editors of the *Dispatch* and the *Messenger* continually constructed their editorials around the threat of "negro domination" and images of sexualized African American males. Ultimately, Alexander Manly became the representative of all of these threats.

In his narrative, "A Statement of the Facts Concerning the Bloody Riot in Wilmington, N.C.," Rev. J. Allen Kirk, D.D., an African American pastor of the Central Baptist Church in Wilmington, reveals how the editorials in the white press reached various elements of white Wilmington society:

There was a request made on the part of the editor of the Wilmington *Daily Messenger* to all of the white ministers of the various denominations of Wilmington, to preach from a certain text on a certain Sabbath before the election and the dire bloody riot, which seemed to agitate and move the people to reek out their sentiments coming from the bosom of the editor and not the text in its biblical connection with the scriptures . . . . The white ministers of Wilmington, N.C. carried their guns in the bloody riot.[37]

Without the protection of the law or the church and without weapons, Manly and other members of the black middle class were forced to leave even the black sections of the city. Numerous documents speculate about his escape, although it is clear that his appearance facilitated his escape.[38]

In fact, Manly rode out of the city unaccosted by members of the white militia who were charged with finding him.

Part of the reason why the white hysteria was so effective was because of the success of the African American middle class in Wilmington. While most major cities had segregated business districts, Main Street in Wilmington was home to numerous African American businesses. There was also an extensive black business district on Seventh Street. The economic and political success of the African American population was the primary focus of the campaign to galvanize the white community against "negro domination." The ensuing hysteria enabled the white populace to envision their actions not as "a mob but a Wilmington army of vindication of Wilmington's social security." [39]

Given the body of evidence supporting the fact that the violence was the direct result of white racialized ululation, it seems ridiculous, as most treatises about the incident do, to credit Manly with starting the race riot.[40] Rather, the architects of Wilmington's white riot needed to incite a white riot to ensure an unchallenged Democratic win in the election.

Ironically, Clawson's memoir reveals information about the beginning of the white riot in Wilmington. This excerpt from his "recollections and memories" is worth quoting at length because it epitomizes the psychotropic effects of white hysteria:

The memory of that machine gun outfit is ineffaceable. It constitutes a recollection I shall never forget. The fiery big horses drawing the outfit were cutting corners and racing at a rapid rate through every section of Brooklyn. It was really a dramatic and thrilling spectacle . . . .

In all about ten or twelve negroes lost their lives in the riot, while two white men were seriously wounded.

The vital feature of the so-called "Revolution" in Wilmington was to stop uncontrolled bloodshed and to restore order. Saving life by heroic action and courage was the crowning event of a direful human calamity. All the heroism was displayed, and planning carried out, before any subsequent event occurred to make November 10th, and 11th, 1898, historic days in the gripping annals of this historic Cape Fear city.

It has always impressed the writer that the machine gun squad was the most available means of getting to the danger spots in a rapid way, when mounted then behind swiftly moving horses, instead of the motor mounted outfits like these of the present day and times. Colonel [Roger] Moore and Captain Kenan, with their men, were on the field with a flying machine-gun squadron, getting at strategic points, when dire emergency made that service a matter of the greatest importance.

On the morning of November 10th, when the party of men led by Colonel A.M. Waddell, destroyed the negro newspaper plant, the riot . . . started.[41]

As is characteristic of press accounts of the era, Clawson imagines the black male bodies the rioters target as being prodigious, focusing on their ability to withstand the two-day Gatling gun assault. He also portrays black riot victims as agents in the exchange while simultaneously portraying his white counterparts as participants in "a vindication." [42] Most important, however, Clawson documents the fact that a white riot, not a "race riot," occurred in Wilmington in his description of the precise moment that the riot began.

Other evidence, particularly with respect to the reports concerning the number of deaths, points to the extent the historical record was altered in newspaper articles about the incident. The majority presses indicate that fewer than ten people were killed in the rioting. [43] However, other historical accounts concur with African American records of the violence. Kirk's record of the event characterizes this:

> It was a great sight to see them [white women and children] marching from death, and the colored women, colored men, colored children, colored enterprises and colored people all exposed to death. Firing began, and it seemed like a mighty battle in war time. The shrieks and screams of children, of mothers, of wives were heard, such as caused the blood of the most unhuman person to creep. Thousands of women, children and men rushed to the swamps and there lay upon the earth in the cold to freeze and starve. The woods were filled with colored people. The streets were dotted with their dead bodies. A white gentleman said that he saw ten bodies lying in the undertakers [*sic*] office at one time. Some of their bodies were left lying in the streets until up in the next day following the riot. Some were found by the stench and miasma that came forth from their decaying bodies. . . . [44]

This horrific chronicle is their only eulogy. There are indications that many of the victims may have been buried in unmarked mass graves or that their bodies were never recovered. Those who were buried in marked grave sites rest in the city-maintained Pine Forest Cemetery where the graves are inaccessible and virtually untended. [45] Adelaide Peterson, the African American woman whose narrative opens this discussion, "came across several dead and others dying from the night's exposure." [46] In keeping with the tradition of displacing the impact of white aggression, the white presses vowed that they would never report an accurate account of the casualties. [47]

Any assessment of the events in Wilmington shows that the riot could not have been easily linked to the publication of Manly's editorial alone. In fact, the Populist Movement that realigned political groups in the South in the early 1890s actually marked the initiation of agitation by the white press. In 1894, a Fusion ticket of predominately black Republicans and

Populists resulted in a change in the municipal government of the city. After this election the city of Wilmington, like many other southern cities, had its first African American appointed officials. The reaction of the old guard marked the initial utterances of racialized ululation, many of which co-incided with the origin of the Fusion ticket with its election of Republicans and "negroes." One broadside entitled "Five Lessons for North Carolina Voters" articulated this by counting the number of African American elected officials, defining the era in terms of "negro domination." It is indicative of the racially emotive publications of the era:

Question—Is there any party in the State composed entirely of white men?
Answer—Yes. The Democratic Party is composed entirely of white men.
Question—Is there any party in the State composed of a majority of negroes?
Answer—Yes, the Republican party has about 115,000 negro voters and about
    30,000 white voters—nearly four negroes to every white man.
Question—Which is the white party, and which the negro party?
Answer—An idiot can answer this question. To every negro in the State the answer
    is easy . . . .
Question—In what way do negroes propose to secure negro supremacy in North
    Carolina?
Answer—By voting the Republican Fusion ticket.
Question—In what way only can white men secure white supremacy in North Carolina?
    lina?
Answer—By voting the Democratic ticket, supported by 155,000 white men.[48]

This text eroticizes the political by emphasizing the power of black sexuality. The sexual power of the "negro" is called forth in the white psyche when the issue of integration, given the racial composition of the Republican Party, is figured as miscegenation, given its threat of "negro supremacy." This broadside presents a deliberate mutation of genetic dominance with political power. One should also note that the writers further titillate their white audience by playing with the relationships between purity and domination in the piece. Designed to heighten white hysteria and simultaneously erase class conflicts, the broadside inscribes white culture as classless and morally pure. In arguing for the existence of this mythologized white culture, the writer exalts white racial purity while denouncing the political miscegenation of the Republican Party. This article is indicative of how white hysteria was encouraged as election day approached. In this climate of white hysteria, A. L. Manly provided the counter-expression to white agitation. It is in this same tradition that Charles Chesnutt revises Wilmington's riot history by making the white riot visible in *The Marrow of Tradition*.

CHESNUTT'S *THE MARROW OF TRADITION*:
UNMASKING WHITE RIOT

It seems clear that Charles Chesnutt wrote *The Marrow of Tradition* to expose Wilmington's white riot and to coalesce the calls for justice that arose from the African American survivors of the riot and their families. His closeness to the racial and social nexus of Wilmington sparked his interest in writing a novel or short story concerning it. In fact as early as 1899, Chesnutt began to frame the plot of the novel, recording two versions of the core story both of which center on a black physician in the midst of a white riot. The short story plot focuses on a "colored professional" who settles in the South "where he can be of more direct use to his people, personally as well as by example."[49] A physician and drugstore owner, this character loses everything to the white riot: his wife (or child), his business, and his home. At the end of the story, as is true of *Marrow*, Chesnutt's doctor is called upon to save the child of the principal white agitator. After he does so, however, he leaves the city declining "white man's protection," preferring "the rights and opportunities of a man."[50] The second protoplot for *Marrow*, which Chesnutt titles "Race Riot Story," climaxes as the doctor reveals the dead body of his child, the victim of the white riot. Again Chesnutt ends with the doctor leaving the southern city; however, in this version he leaves in a Jim Crow car to portray the racial delusions of American apartheid. Yet despite the militancy of the endings of these early versions of the novel, the ending of *The Marrow of Tradition* finds Chesnutt's protagonist, Dr. William Miller, saving the life of the chief antagonist's son, leaving his wife alone to mourn the loss of their only child. Readers are left to wonder what happens beyond the confines of the novel. The novel's ending, in fact, seems to require some rationalization of the good doctor's willingness to subsume his grief in order to save the heir to the white supremacist ululation. Like his "conjah" stories, the novel simultaneously portrays the horror of white supremacy and the tenacity of black survival. And despite the fact that the novel was published only three years after the white riot, Chesnutt is able to capture the racially charged event, using characters that are readily identifiable as some of white Wilmington's most prominent citizens. Certainly the novel is a protest against the white riot with Chesnutt all but naming the participants in the violence in his thinly veiled portraits of the conspirators. Yet for all of its militancy, the close of *Marrow* begs questions about Dr. Miller's—and certainly Chesnutt's—stance on black social equality or black acceptance of white racist practice. What should the contemporary reader of the novel have seen in the ending, so seemingly incomplete? And what does Chesnutt's decision to leave Miller's future in limbo—especially given the endings of the protoplots—mean in a novel that, as I shall discuss, is otherwise exceedingly clear about white riot?

It should be clear from Chesnutt's *Marrow* and from Thorne's *Hanover* that protest is at the core of African American historical fiction about riot events. *Hanover* received little contemporary critical attention, probably due to the fact that he openly based his account on witness narratives of the event. Inevitably, it was easily silenced in the same manner in which the white rioters silenced the black press. The protest tradition, however, centers on the fictionalization of historical events. In this vein Charles Chesnutt, unlike any other author of his period, uses the novel form to recover the true history of the riot. This impulse is evident in the fictionalized unraveling of the events surrounding the Wilmington violence in 1898. With the only voice of African American society in Wilmington silenced by the departure of Manly and other politically powerful African Americans, the preservation of the historical record was relegated to the province of literature. In *The Marrow of Tradition,* Chesnutt uses fiction to make Wilmington's white riot visible.

Klaus Ensslen indicates that although a preoccupation with history is central in African American literature, history remains veiled.[51] However, particularly given the culture of racism surrounding the early 1900s, Chesnutt is decidedly exact in detailing the events of the massacre, for his is not the story of a black "race riot," but is rather a correction of the historical narratives inscribed by majority annals. In *The Marrow of Tradition,* Chesnutt immerses the reader in the experience of Wilmington 1898, signifying on the distorted histories of the riot event.

Chesnutt was, in fact, situated close to the events in Wilmington in 1898, having grown up in Fayetteville, North Carolina, at a time when the Yadkin Valley and Cape Fear Railway linked the cities. Chesnutt's use of the train to introduce the reader to the narrative is indicative of his ability to focus on the complexities of race in both the novel and in American culture. Indeed, the railroad has always been a symbol of America's racial schizophrenia. In African American literature, references to trains and the railroad recall the racial divide implicit in a variety of discourses on race. Railroads marked the dividing line between black and white America, from providing the line of demarcation between segregated communities to the existence of Jim Crow cars. The Jim Crow cars were the space in which Pullman porters found both economic opportunity and racial subjugation. They represented racial difference, especially as it was shaped in the laws governing race between the North and the South. The rail system, in

essence, was the marker of the differences between America's racial promise and its racial practices. In *Marrow,* Chesnutt focuses on the railroad as a
symbol of America's racial divide, immersing the reader in the racist praxis
of his fictional city, Wellington. Interestingly, the name of his fictional city
resonates with the racial politics of Wilmington as well as with a racial confrontation in the Chesnutt family history. Chesnutt's father, Andrew, was
among members of the African American community who confronted the
slave hunters in Wellington, Ohio.[52] Evoking the Fugitive Slave Law, the
slave hunters tried to abduct one of the members of the African American
community. Commemorating the racist practices his family remembered
from Wellington, Ohio, Chesnutt's fictional Wellington is a city in which
racial lines are both impassable, given the protagonist's treatment under the
Jim Crow laws, and transient, since these "laws," both in transportation
and through miscegenation, are often crossed.

Marrow's train scene exposes the complexity of the color line which
Chesnutt conveys through multiple images: the communal relationship between his black protagonist, William Miller, and his white colleague, Dr.
Alvin Burns; Miller's seeming acceptance of racial stereotyping; and his
description of Josh Greene, Miller's dark, working-class reflection. All of
these images come together on the train, the image that has long been a
symbol of racial intolerance in African American literature. Chesnutt com-
bines powerful symbolism of the train with the power of the press as he
describes the encounter between Miller and Burns on the train. As Chesnutt notes in this scene, race "is a tremendously interesting problem. It is
a serial story which we are all reading, and which grows in vital interest
with each successive installment." [53] Chesnutt reiterates this fusion of racial
ideology and the press after Miller is forced to move to the colored car. Although this scene is lengthy, I include it because it emphasizes the impact of
race ideology and the power of the press at this particular cultural moment:

The car was conspicuously labeled at either end with large cards, similar to those
in the other car, except that they bore the word "Colored" in black letters upon a
white background. The author of this piece of legislation had contrived, with an in-
genuity worthy of a better cause, that not merely should the passengers be separated
by the color line, but that the reason for this division should be kept constantly in
mind. Lest a white man should forget that he was white,—not a very likely con-
tingency,—these cars would keep him constantly admonished of the fact; should a
colored person endeavor, for a moment, to lose sight of his disability, these staring
signs should remind him continually that between him and the rest of mankind not
of his own color, there was by law a great gulf fixed.

Having composed himself, Miller had opened a newspaper, and was deep in
an editorial which set forth in glowing language the inestimable advantages which

would follow to certain recently acquired islands by the introduction of American liberty, when the rear door of the car opened to give entrance to Captain George McBane, who took a seat near the door and lit a cigar. . . . He represented the aggressive element among the white people of the New South, who made it hard for a negro to maintain his self-respect or to enjoy even the rights conceded to colored men by Southern laws. McBane had undoubtedly identified him to the conductor in the other car.[54]

Not only does Chesnutt emphasize the mutability of Jim Crow laws in this passage, he emphasizes the mutability of race. If blackness as it is understood in the racialized ululation of the moment is so conspicuous, it should not have been necessary for Miller to have been identified. Racial identity is again challenged on the train in Miller's own racial ideology which he articulates after the colored car is filled with farm laborers "fresh from their daily toil."[55]

Indicative of Chesnutt's methods in this section, the newspaper is again the point of reference that defines the racial and political climate about which he writes:

By and by, however, the air became too close, and he went out upon the platform. For the sake of the democratic ideal, which meant so much to his race, he might have endured the affliction. He could easily imagine that people of refinement, with the power in their hands, might be tempted to strain the democratic ideal in order to avoid such contact; but personally and apart from the mere matter of racial sympathy, these people were just as offensive to him as to the whites in the other end of the train. . . . It was a veritable bed of Procrustes, this standard which the whites had set for the negroes. Those who grew above it must have their heads cut off, figuratively speaking, — must be forced back to the level assigned to their race; those who fell beneath the standards had their necks stretched, literally enough, as the ghastly record in the daily papers gave conclusive evidence.[56]

Through such intersections of the train and memory, the press and reality, and "evidence" and ideology, Chesnutt prepares the reader for a journey toward a revisioning of history. *Marrow* provides the counter-text to the historical record that bears the trace of the racialized ululation. In *Marrow* he fuses the historical with the fictional as a means of resistance against the majority historical record. In this, the last of Chesnutt's fictional work to be published during his lifetime, he reconstructs the Wilmington of 1898 in the guise of Wellington, North Carolina, using a number of contemporary references to redress the history of the event.

Chesnutt appropriates the written discourse about Wilmington to construct a narrative about race, class, and violence in his fictional Wellington. Chesnutt's *Marrow* unveils the polemics of the racialized representations

of the event by accurately representing the class and race dynamics that
lead to the white riot. He also provides a teleology of the unrest, including
highlighting the white supremacist conspiracy and the pattern of weapons
distribution in his fictionalized version of Wilmington in 1898.

While Ensslen suggests that African American historical fiction written around the turn of the century remains veiled and "not especially con-
ducive to a more or less explicit challenging of official versions of history,"
Chesnutt's fictionalized history is the exception.[57] Rather than presenting
a veiled discourse about the Wilmington unrest, Chesnutt records a representation of the event that is closer to the complex reality of the society at
the time than are the representations articulated in white versions of the
event. What Chesnutt is revising is the notion of truth that Bakhtin articulates in his theory of "language, no longer [being] as a sacrosanct and soli-
tary embodiment of meaning and truth . . . merely one of many possible
ways to hypothesize meaning."[58] The use of linguistic structures in *Marrow* attests to Chesnutt's view that truth and meaning are integral to the
project of African American historical fiction. In the novel Chesnutt uses
the history of orature and of inscription to revise the texts of 1898 Wil-
mington/Wellington, making it symbolic of the prevailing notions about
race, class, and sex in 1898 Wilmington and in the United States as a whole.
It is clear from this proximity and the unfolding of the events in *Marrow*
that Chesnutt also attempts to replicate events about which he has primary
knowledge. Chesnutt's integration of history and fiction is shaped by his
attention to the various cultural representations at work in the documentation of the historical event.

Chesnutt's depiction of Wilmington/Wellington stresses the relationships between the multiple histories that comprise the riot scene: remembered versions of class and race structure that are buried in African American narrative accounts, the discourse of class and race manufactured in the
racialized ululation in Wilmington in 1898 and in the United States as a
whole, and the inaccessible historical record that the latter attempts to subvert. Chesnutt encodes the novel with the various truths of these dividend
discourses.

It is at this juncture that the roles of African American literature and
the press converge. As previously noted only two copies of the *Record* sur-
vived the violence; neither of them contains the editorial around which the
civil unrest was constructed. Chesnutt, like his predecessor Harriet Wilson,
chose to revision published versions of these events in his novel *Marrow*.
Interwoven into the story of the riot, Chesnutt provides the reader with
a historical format through which to consider the "fictionalized" events.

This rewriting of history questions the press accounts of the event, placing "truth" in the province of the literary imagination rather than in editorialized versions incumbent to the process of white racialized ululation. Chesnutt exposes the problems in the social order as they revolve around constructions and conceptions of race and class. To explore Chesnutt's view of the connection between history and African American literature, note how he characterizes the role of the writer in his journal in 1880:

This work is of a two-fold character. The Negro's part is to prepare himself for recognition and equality, and it is the province of literature to open the way for him to get it—to accustom the public mind to the idea; to lead people out, imperceptibly, unconsciously, step by step, to the desired state of feeling. If I can do anything to further this work, and can see any likelihood of obtaining success in it, I would gladly devote my life to it.[59]

Chesnutt reveals a political motivation for writing literature. Although he published stories about the race problem in the United States under other titles, *Marrow* is one of only two works in which he fictionalizes a specific historic event.[60] Yet how does his fictionalization of a historic event assume the political dimension of being able to "accustom the mind" to such an idea? Chesnutt's ability to integrate the untold history of the African American riot experience in Wilmington is like his impetus to write of "a two-fold character."[61] Writing to "accustom the public mind" about the events necessitated that Chesnutt align himself with the riot survivors who could witness to the African American presence within the riot. Among them were prominent members of the white community, exiled African Americans, and Dr. Thomas R. Mask, who like Chesnutt's fictional Dr. Miller, "survives" the riot and remains in Wilmington. The other reason that compelled Chesnutt to write about the Wilmington's white riot involves a curious unfolding of the textual relationship between Chesnutt's stories and the riot events.

As indicated, the events Chesnutt fictionalizes in Wellington are, in part, derived from Chesnutt's relationships with survivors of the riot. Chesnutt's description of Dr. Miller's ride through Wellington in the novel are in fact based on the riot experiences of Dr. Thomas R. Mask, the third African American doctor to practice in Wilmington. There are a few clues as to the nature or extent of their friendship. Chesnutt's uncle, Dallas Chesnutt, also resided in Wilmington, one block from the Mask's home and on the same street as Alexander Manly.[62] Chesnutt hints at their relationship in a letter dated 11 November 1905 written to Mrs. W. E. Henderson, the wife of another African American survivor of the Wilmington riot. Chesnutt writes:

The book was suggested by the Wilmington riot, with the date and details of which you are more familiar than I am, since it was the occasion of your husband's leaving the South.

I am unable to retrace the process by which the book grew, it was suggested by a vivid description given me by Dr. Mask, during a visit of his to Cleveland, of the events of the riot and a ride which he took across the city during its progress. The personal element of the story is what the most of any novel must be—the fruit of my own imagination.[63]

Dr. Mask, as I shall fully explore, becomes the prototype for Chesnutt's protagonist, William Miller. Further, Chesnutt's connection with other riot survivors is exemplified in his knowledge of how the riot affected Henderson's exile. Because he is able to voice the experience of the riot survivors, Chesnutt's chronicle of the events in Wilmington is his attempt to recolorize the monoracial history of the riot.

Chesnutt's visits to North Carolina after the violence enable him to integrate the riot experiences of both the African American community as well as that part of the white community that opposed the violence in Wilmington. Chesnutt's correspondence reveals that he was also well acquainted with the family of James Sprunt. Sprunt, though one of the wealthiest white businessmen in Wilmington at the time of the riot, reportedly armed himself to defend his African American employees from an attack by Wilmington's white rioters. During the winter of 1900, Chesnutt visited with Sprunt and J. E. Garford, the collector of customs, who describes his relationship with Chesnutt as "a fellowship."[64] This close association with the riot witnesses from both racial communities enables Chesnutt to revision the social milieu of Wilmington as he historicizes the events of the riot in the novel.

What might be the most intimate piece of the interrelationship between Chesnutt and the events in Wilmington in 1898 is the intertextuality between the event and Chesnutt's work. Wholly without Chesnutt's permission, Manly serialized *The Wife of His Youth* in the *Record*. Perhaps these stories with their emphasis on the mutability of the color line would have been just as volatile, just as racially and sexually transgressing, as the Manly editorial. What is clear, however, is the intimacy between the reprinting of the collection and the riot. Chesnutt alludes to this in a letter to Thomas Hines Page, then Chesnutt's editor at Houghton Mifflin & Company:

I am deeply concerned and very much depressed at the condition of affairs in North Carolina during the campaign. I have been for a long time praising the State for its superior fairness and liberality in the treatment of race questions, but I find myself obliged to revise some of my judgments. There is absolutely no excuse for

Dr. Thomas R. Mask's tombstone. Charles Chesnutt based his portrayal of the white riot in Wilmington on the eyewitness account of Dr. Mask.

the state of things there, for the State has a very large white majority. It is an outbreak of pure, malignant and altogether indefensible race prejudice, which makes me feel [Chesnutt writes "ashamed of" and marks it out] personally humiliated and ashamed for the country and the State. The United States Government is apparently powerless, and the recent occurrences in Illinois in connection with the miners' strike seem to emphasize its weakness.

But I should not inflict my views on you in this matter, except of a circumstance you may find interesting. The colored people's newspaper, *The Daily Record*, the office of which was burned yesterday by a mob of the "best citizens" of Wilmington, numbering in their ranks many "ministers of the gospel" and the editor of which has been compelled to flee for his life, republished "The Wife of His Youth" in installments running over about a week, sometime ago, and somebody sent me several copies of the paper. It gave credit to the *Atlantic*, but I rather doubted whether it had obtained your permission to copy the story. If I had the heart to joke on a subject that seems to me very seriously and hopelessly tragical, I might say that misfortunes of the newspaper were a sort of divine retribution, or poetic justice for a violation of copyright.[65]

It is perhaps the intertextual relationship between Chesnutt's writing and the violence that provides the impetus for Chesnutt's literary exploration of the riot. The insistence on revising the text of the riot becomes evident in Chesnutt's scheme of naming in remembering the event, all the while challenging the prevailing social history by this signification. As Henry Louis Gates, Jr., notes in his articulation of signifying, the topos of naming is integral to African American culture; it also is integral to Chesnutt's project in *Marrow*.[66] Naming is the principle method that Chesnutt uses to imbue the novel with the textual representations of truth. In his insistence on revising the historical text of the events, Chesnutt calls the participants in the racialized ululation "out of their names," while at the same time he names their place in the cultural and political milieu. Although the true name remains unspoken, the name is remembered habitually because the identities of the white rioters had been established in the various memoirs and press accounts of the violence.[67]

In a style atypical from that which he employs in *The Wife of His Youth* and *The House behind the Cedars*, Chesnutt delays describing the community of Wellington/Wilmington until chapter 16. This perhaps attests to how he is able to publish the text so soon after the event, even though it is clear from the "race riots" which occur with increasing intensity through 1919 that his topic is potentially volatile. He characterizes Wellington as being in the midst of economic change: "Twenty years before, Wellington had been the world's greatest shipping port for naval sources. But as the turpentine industry had moved southward, leaving a trail of devastated forests in its rear, the city had fallen to a poor fifth or sixth place in this trade, relying now almost entirely upon cotton for its export business."[68] Although Chesnutt does not relate specific events about the location of Wellington, the un-naming he utilizes in the text is sufficient to characterize both the location and the economic condition of Wilmington in 1898. The economic conditions foregrounded in the description of Wellington match the declining economic base of Wilmington 1898. In 1878, Wilmington marketed 154,985 barrels of crude turpentine; however, as early as 1883, production dropped 60 percent. During the same period, cotton receipts increased, and by 1883 cotton exports rose dramatically.[69] The result was the need to mobilize a labor force for cotton production, a process which relied heavily upon hand-labor. The large African American population in Wilmington was indicative of the shift in African American labor patterns. Though subtle, Chesnutt's description of the economic conditions of Wilmington/Wellington provides a means to read race and class matters in terms of a shifting economy that must return to an agrarian base for profit, a base that would depend upon the return of large numbers of black bodies to the cotton fields. In this singular reference Chesnutt names the underlying economic reasons for the social cataclysm that shapes both the white riot and the novel.

Though buried in the subplot of the novel, this reference about Wellington is also significant because of its placement. The description is woven into the subplot of the novel that depicts the devolution of the southern white aristocracy in the person of Tom Delamere. Delamere murders Polly Ochiltree, an acerbic old woman born into the southern white aristocracy, and frames his father's servant, Sandy, "an exception to any rule which you may formulate in derogation of the negro servant," for her death.[70] Chesnutt so constructs the tone of the murder subplot that it is not immediately apparent how it figures in his revision of the historical text. Note, however, how the subplot characterizes a Wellington incensed by a racialized ululation constructed around a disruption in what I term as the cult of white womanhood:

No sooner was the verdict announced than the community, or at least the white third of it, resolved itself spontaneously into a committee of the whole to discover the perpetrator of the dastardly crime, which, at this stage of the affair, seemed merely one of robbery and murder.

Suspicion was at once directed toward the negroes, as it always is when an unexplained crime is committed in a Southern community . . . .

The whole race, in the major's opinion, was morally undeveloped, and only held within bounds by the restraining influence of the white people. Under Mr. Delamere's thumb, this Sandy had been a model servant,—faithful, docile, respectful, and self-respecting. . . . Left to his own degraded ancestral instincts, Sandy had begun to deteriorate, and a rapid decline had culminated in this robbery and murder,—and who knew what other horror? The criminal was a negro, the victim a white woman;—it was only reasonable to expect the worst.

"He'll swing for it," observed the general.[71]

Chesnutt's inclusion of this scene in the novel underscores the charge that is used against the Manly editorial: that Manly "slanders" white women and

"excuses rapists." [72] He also underscores Manly's assertion that the race of
an alleged criminal is sufficient to equate the crime to that of rape, with
the lynching of the "big, burly, black brute" the necessary result. Chesnutt,
then, blends the fictive and the historical records encoding the novel with
the kind of racialized ululation that preceded Wilmington's white riot.

In addition to signifying on the community in the novel, Chesnutt explores coded cultural constructions of race in the text. He uses the novel to
articulate conflicting notions about race traits from divergent sources. In so
doing Chesnutt inscribes the notion of race as a socially constructed text,
a text written into the historical record of Wilmington. Maj. Carteret's
aspersions about the "degraded ancestral instincts" of African Americans
becomes significant because of the actual identity of the murderer. Tom
Delamere is a character in blackface. [73] In Delamere, Chesnutt constructs
a white character capable of affecting Sandy's habits, thereby questioning
the culture's reading of whiteness. As Eric Lott suggests, minstrelsy marks
the black male body sexually and as a sign of white guilt. [74] And Chesnutt's
portrait of Thomas Delamere as a minstrel presence suggests something
peculiar about the power of white privilege, whose existence relies upon
the ability to shift blame from one racial body to the other.

Blackness, whiteness, and the "shocking mésalliance," of the two are
the foci of Chesnutt's study of white riot. [75] Evoking Manly's use of miscegenation in his editorial, Chesnutt creates black characters that force racial
re-readings in the course of the novel. I have previously noted that Miller
had to be identified in the whites-only car on the train by McBane, one of
the participants in the conspiracy to incite the riot. Chesnutt also includes
other "white" blacks in the novel, including Janet Miller, whose body is,
as I shall discuss later, the ultimate racial text. Aside from the construction of blackness in terms of miscegenation and white minstrelsy, Chesnutt includes Jane and Jerry Letlow, characters who are closely allied to the
whites, who are descendants of their former owners. Taken in terms of the
white community's opinion of them, their blackness is an ideal, one that
the entire "race" should follow. Chesnutt offers an alternate view of their
blackness given their conscious decision to remain in a state of voluntary
slavery. In essence, Chesnutt heightens her disconnectedness to African tradition in his characterization of Mammy Jane. Although Sundquist casts
Mammy Jane as a conjure woman, "at odds with Miller's classical medical
training," [76] I argue that Chesnutt describes her in precisely the opposite
way. Indeed, Jane has no primary knowledge of African cultural practices.
Chesnutt underscores her lack of black cultural connectedness in his description of Jane's "conjuring" ritual:

Jane's duties in the nursery did not permit her to visit her friend the conjure woman; but she did find time to go out in the back yard at dusk, and to dig up the charm which she had planted there. It had protected the child so far; but perhaps its potency had become exhausted. She picked up the bottle, shook it vigorously, and then laid it back, with the other side up. Refilling the hole, she made a cross over the top with the thumb of her left hand, and walked three times around it.

What this strange symbolism meant, or whence it derived its origin, Aunt Jane did not know. The cross was there, and the Trinity, though Jane was scarcely conscious of these, at this moment, as religious symbols.[77]

Shackled to white supremacy and disassociated from any vestige of blackness, Jane is unable to recognize the symbology of her ancestral roots. Mammy Jane straddles the world of black and white, belonging to neither tradition. For Chesnutt, Jane represents white supremacist notions of blackness. Mammy Jane is the exaggeration of blackness that confirms their notions about race difference. Further, she embraces whiteness in her literal and cultural disassociation with even the rituals of her "race." Chesnutt re-creates these coded cultural notions about race, thereby embedding the novel with the racialized ululation that preceded Wilmington's white riot.

Not surprisingly, Chesnutt also explores the ways in which class issues propel white racialized violence and the white riot that follows. This is neither the first time nor the last in which racial violence has erupted with this kind of devastating results in segregated communities. The Irish population of Wilmington, led by Mike Dowling, also participated in the violence. Dowling, one of the unemployed underclass is described as "both the organizer and the leader of the Redshirts."[78] Chesnutt includes class-race strife in the novel in the chapter aptly entitled "Mine Enemy, O Mine Enemy." The following passage reflects how class becomes a "character" in the text:

The crowd, too surrounding the hospital, had changed somewhat in character. The men who had acted as leaders in the early afternoon, having accomplished their purpose of overturning the local administration and establishing a provisional government of their own, had withdrawn from active participation in the rioting, deeming the negroes already sufficiently overawed to render unlikely any further trouble from that source. . . . The baser element of the white population, recruited from the wharves and the saloons, was now predominant. . . .

On the outskirts of the crowd a few of the better class, or at least of the better clad, were looking on.[79]

It is easy to see here that Chesnutt plays with the ways that race, class, ethnicity, and gender converge at the center of the unrest. That this con-

struction persists in more recent race/class violence is clarified by the Los
Angeles unrest in 1992. Robert Reinhold, reporting for the *New York Times*
on 3 May 1992 at the height of the 1992 Los Angeles Rebellion, emphasizes
this legacy in his assertion that when "the middle class leaves . . . ethnic
groups are pitted against one another."[80] This statement characterizes the
race violence from the turn of the century to the present.

Chesnutt weaves notions of race and class together in his inclusion of
the conspiracy plot in the novel. If, as the discourse of racialized ululation
both in Chesnutt's text and the historical record insists, the violence is the
result of white righting of the social and political climate, then the conspiracy plot also debunks the notion that the violence was necessary. In his
inclusion of the conspiracy plot early in the novel, Chesnutt is the first to remember the violence in these terms. Chesnutt, however, places limitations
on the narrative in order for it to survive as a "telling" text.[81] The white supremacist conspirators in Wilmington use the press to summon the wave of
violence. In the novel, Chesnutt assembles a committee known as the "Big
Three" composed of Philip Carteret, the editor of the Democratic press;
Captain George McBane, a nouveau riche descendent of the "poor-white
class"; and General Belmont, a lawyer who "takes an active role in state
and local politics."[82] What Chesnutt tells in the conspiracy plot is the un-
written version of how the riot is constructed. The table opposite chronicles
the riot with Chesnutt's reconstruction of the event. As the chronology indicates, Chesnutt's *Marrow* is the story of a white riot. In his inclusion of
these details in the text, he signifies on the historical events point by point.

In the novel, Chesnutt clearly uses the topos of *un*naming to identify
the principal agitators in the white riot. Undoubtedly, he calls the cast of
historical characters "out of their names" yet identifies each one or them
clearly. As I see it, Chesnutt does not veil the identities of their historical
counterparts in order to indict the white rioters.[83] General Belmont, described as "a dapper little gentleman with light blue eyes and a Vandyke
beard,"[84] is "a lawyer by profession, and took an active part in state and
local politics."[85] Aside from his Confederate rank, Chesnutt's Belmont is
described exactly as Alfred M. Waddell is in the journals of the era. Ex-
congressman Waddell is described in *Collier's Weekly* as a typical southern gentleman, "a descendant of the genuine aristocracy . . . of average
height, thin, and always immaculately dressed. . . . with a full and well-kept
beard."[86] Chesnutt further inscribes this association in his description of
Philip Carteret, who, as editor of the fictive *Chronicle* in the text, is the fictive characterization of Thomas Clawson, editor of the *Wilmington Daily
Messenger*. In addition to Carteret's description, the history of the *Chronicle*

A chronological comparison of Wilmington, North Carolina, 1898, and Charles Chesnutt's fictional town of Wellington from *The Marrow of Tradition*.

Wilmington 1898	Chesnutt's Wellington
Manly editorial printed in the *Record* on 18 August 1898.	*Banner* article appears. (85)
Press campaign of white supremacy intensifies up to the November elections.	"That editorial in the negro newspaper is good campaign matter, but we should reserve it until it will be most effective. Suppose we just stick it in a pigeon-hole, and let the editor . . . hang himself. In the mean time we will continue to work up public opinion, . . and when the state campaign opens we'll print the editorial, with suitable comment, scatter it broadcast throughout the state . . . have a little demonstration with red shirts and shotguns, [and] scare the negroes into fits . . . ." (89)
"For a period of six to twelve months prior to November 10th, 1898, the white citizens of Wilmington prepared quietly but effectively for the day when action would be necessary." [a]	"The campaign was fought along the color line." (240)
Manly editorial reprinted November 1898.	"A peg was needed upon which to hang a coup d'état, and this editorial offered the requisite opportunity. It was unanimously decided to republish the obnoxious article, with comment adapted to fire the inflammable Southern heart and rouse it against any further self-assertion of the negroes in politics or elsewhere." (243)
"[T]he Norfolk merchants have been shipping firearms to the Old North State for the past thirty days. . . . "We learn that the caliber of the guns bought are for hunting purposes, [and] would be used only to shoot bear or buffalo." [b]	"[N]o white merchant would sell a negro fire arms . . . . The white people, on the other hand procured both arms and ammunition in large quantities." (248)
"The Wilmington Race Riot occurred on the morning of November 10th 1898 . . . . a number of determined citizens . . . set the [*Record*] building afire." [c]	"The Wellington riot began at three o'clock in the afternoon of a day as fair as was ever selected for a deed of darkness." (274)

[a] Thomas Clawson, "The Wilmington Race Riot in 1898: Recollections and Memories," Louis T. Moore Papers, New Hanover County Collection, North Carolina Department of Archives and History, Raleigh, N.C., 1.

[b] "Guns Still Coming to N.C.," *Wilmington Evening Dispatch,* 7 November 1898, 4.

[c] Clawson, 2–3.

reveals the extent to which Chesnutt went to connect his characters to their historical counterparts. A *Wilmington Chronicle* was established as a Whig press in 1838. In 1851, the press was sold to Talcott Burr, and the name was changed to the *Wilmington Herald*. Two years after Burr's death in 1858, his heirs sold the press to A. M. Waddell.[87] This is the kind of cyclical inscribing that Chesnutt continues in reference to the *Record*, which he calls the *Afro-American Banner* in *Marrow*.[88]

It seems, though, that through the portraitures of his African American characters Chesnutt completely revises the text of the white riot by giving voice to the part of society that the white riot attempted to silence. The "impudent nigger"[89] who runs the *Banner* is seemingly relegated to a mere mention in the text. "The nigger's name is Barber,"[90] yet Chesnutt provides no physical description of the character. In the naming of the other characters and of the city of Wellington, Chesnutt provides physical, cyclical, and social clues. Yet it is not immediately clear how Chesnutt provides the link between Manly and Barber aside from their occupations. In the naming of Barber, Chesnutt establishes a link between the racialized ululation in Wellington with the racial agitation that characterizes 1898 in the United States as a whole. By the time Chesnutt publishes *Marrow* in 1901, "race riots" have already occurred in numerous cities in the United States: in 1866 in Memphis, Tennessee; in 1866 in New Orleans, Louisiana; in 1873 in Colfax, Louisiana; in 1874 in Hamburg, South Carolina; in 1883 in Danville, Virginia; in 1898 in Wilmington, North Carolina, and Phoenix, South Carolina; and in 1900 in New Orleans, Louisiana, and in New York, New York.[91] African American editors, in particular, bear the brunt of the racialized violence because they necessarily become the spokespeople for the disenfranchised. Like Eric Sundquist, I am convinced that Chesnutt names Barber as a tribute to an established African American editor whose fate mirrored that of Barber in *Marrow*. Jesse Max Barber, as editor of Atlanta's *Voice of the Negro* in 1906, was forced to relocate to Chicago after writing an editorial about the causes of the Atlanta riot; he had a long-standing reputation as a "radical editor."[92] Barber's journalistic reputation had already been established at Virginia Union where he edited the school newspaper. He was hired as coeditor of the *Voice* in 1903 at the age of twenty-five, just a few months after his graduation. By 1904, Barber had also established a professional relationship with Chesnutt. In one of the earliest examples of compensation in the African American press, he paid Chesnutt for an article he contributed to the *Voice*.[93] He edited the *Voice* until 1907, having become the sole editor by 1906. Barber was also later associated with the *Crisis* from its inception in 1910.[94] It is clear that

Chesnutt selected a name from the ranks of black editors in order to signify that the color line separated the nation, rather than just the community of Wilmington in 1898.[95]

This kind of attention to social and historical detail is evident in Chesnutt's depiction of the riot itself. Of the last six chapters in the novel, four present the physical violence of the riot, while the last two concern the psychological violence of miscegenation. Both events relate wholly to attempts to maintain racial separation. Chesnutt views the critical scenes of physical violence through the African American protagonists in the novel, Will Miller and Josh Green. Chesnutt's initial placement of these characters in the train scene illustrates how they reflect one another, mirroring their respective social positions. In his depiction of the riot Chesnutt relates how their disparate social positions contribute to their participation in the violence. Writing in the introduction to the 1969 edition of the novel, Robert Farnsworth indicates that Chesnutt identifies with Miller primarily because the character embodies the possibilities of assimilation and accommodation.[96] However, Chesnutt's commitment to revisioning the historical text and his characterization of Miller resist such an interpretation of Chesnutt's portrayal of Miller. Miller's orientation is familial, rather than social. In Miller, Chesnutt *seems* to create a character with no communal identification to his "race." Note in the exchange between the two protagonists that Miller's commitment is toward his nuclear family while Green's is oriented toward the nucleus of the African American community:

"Hello, doctuh!" cried Josh, "does you wan' ter jine us?"

"I'm looking for my wife and child, Josh. They're somewhere in this den of murderers. Have any of you seen them?"

No one had seen them.

"You men are running a great risk," said Miller. "You are rushing on to certain death."

"Well, suh, maybe we is; but we're gwine ter die fightin'. Dey say de w'ite folks is gwine ter bu'n all de cullud schools an' chu'ches, an' kill de niggers dey kin ketch. Dey're gwine ter bu'n yo' new hospittle, ef somebody don' stop 'em."

"Josh—men—you are throwing your lives away. It is a fever; it will wear off tomorrow, or to-night. . . . They'll only kill the colored people who resist them. . . . Resistance only makes the matter worse,—the odds against you are too long."

". . . Dey're gwine ter kill us anyhow; an' we're tired—we read de newspapers, —an' we're tired er bein' shot down like dogs, without jedge er jury. We'd ruther die fightin' dan be stuck like pigs in a pen!"

"God help you!" said Miller. "As for me, I must find my wife and child."[97]

For Miller the violence is the latest manifestation of the southern order. In his refusal to see beyond the threat to his family, he denies even the plau-

sibility of resistance. It might be argued that Chesnutt uses Miller to question the accommodation affluence often requires. Even in his naming of
this character, Chesnutt challenges the shifting political position of Kelly
Miller who was then the dean of the Liberal Arts School at Howard University. Miller had protested against Booker T. Washington's comments after
the Atlanta Exposition speech of 1875. However, following the Wilmington
violence, Kelly Miller publicly embraced the same political philosophy that
Washington proposed in Atlanta.[98] It may seem, then, that Chesnutt condemns the actions of his protagonist with the same vehemence with which
W. E. B. DuBois attacked the reaction of the Washingtonian black intelli-
gentsia to the racial violence that defined the era.[99]

Despite what seems to be compelling evidence to the contrary, I maintain that Chesnutt's portrait of Dr. Miller is neither one of self-effacement
nor of accommodation. Chesnutt's commitment to recasting the southern
historical text and the detail he supplies about Miller suggest otherwise.
In a city shaped by threat of white riot, Miller manages to negotiate a
pivotal cultural position, being both a "colored" man in the southern tradition and the consummate black professional. While he is riding in the
whites-only car of the Jim Crow train, for instance, Miller has to be *identified* as black. Miller is able to defy white supremacist ideology by refusing to remain in his proper "negro" place. His "black" wife, Janet, is the
physical embodiment of the subversion of the southern understanding of
blackness. Janet Miller and Elizabeth Carteret—the wife of Chesnutt's fictionalized counterpart of Thomas Clawson—are so much alike that their
bodies can replace each other's. As Mammy Jane reveals early in the novel,
they are half-sisters, ". . . ez much like her ez if dey wuz twins. Folks some-
times takes 'em fer one ernudder . . . ."[100] It is important to note that
Miller purchases the ancestral home of Elizabeth Carteret, the icon of white
womanhood in *Marrow*. His acquisition of the house not only demonstrates
Miller's economic success, but it also suggests that Miller has the ability to
threaten the southern aristocracy on its own soil, making his black wife the
legitimate heir to her father's estate. And given that Miller has the power
to save or destroy the life of Carteret's only son at the novel's end, he is
the ultimate witness to this white riot that Chesnutt limns in *The Marrow
of Tradition*. For Miller, racism and the violence that it generates are temporary affectations because they will not continually affect those who, like
him, deny the plausibility of resistance. The key to his position as witness
to the white riot lies in the model on which Chesnutt created the character. The answer lies in Chesnutt's association with Dr. Thomas R. Mask,
whose life is remembered in Chesnutt's Miller.

A native of Rockingham, North Carolina, Thomas Mask graduated from the Leonard Medical School of Shaw University in 1889. One of the first four-year medical schools in the nation, Leonard drew black scholars from all over the world. After his graduation, Mask established a medical practice and drugstore in his wife's home, Wilmington. What made Mask a compelling focus for Chesnutt goes beyond their friendship. Mask was the epitome of the black professional, successful not only in his practice but as a businessman as well. Before his death in 1911, Mask owned over seventy tracts of land in both the black and white sections of the city. Of those tracts, three were purchased the year of the white riot, quite an accomplishment for a black man in a city dominated by monuments to the Confederacy.

Unlike most of the affluent members of the black middle class, Mask remained in Wilmington after the riot. This fact, however, is not a testimony to Mask's accommodation to white supremacy. Perhaps another explanation—and key to Chesnutt's portrait of Miller—is found in Chesnutt's journal. Let me return, then, to the two protoplots which frame Chesnutt's earliest attempts to write about Wilmington's white riot. In one of the story lines Chesnutt indicates that after the doctor saves the life of the son of the principal white agitator, he gains the respect and "protection" of his "new-found friend."[101] While there is no record of Mask having saved the life of such an heir, it does seem likely that he did gain a favorable place in the eyes of the white Democratic elite. His lengthy obituary, published in the white supremacist *Wilmington Morning Star* reads:

He was of the conservative type of the leaders of his race in the South and had done much toward cultivating these relations which should exist between the white and colored peoples of the State and Nation. Endowed with a superior intellect, a man of high character, a master of his profession and with a sense of duty to his people and to his country, he was an exceedingly valuable citizen and his loss will be keenly felt in the community in which he resided. . . .

In addition to being quite proficient as a practitioner, he was a successful business man, a rare combination in the professions, and he had amassed a competency during his life, leaving a large estate . . . .

In business life Dr. Mask was especially well known and yesterday many white citizens took occasion to pay him tribute as to character, honesty, and integrity.[102]

A seemingly impossible feat in a city shaped by white racialized ululation, Mask manages to assume a pivotal cultural position, being both a "colored man" in the southern tradition and the consummate professional. Mask's decision to remain in Wilmington after the white riot is not usually read as militantly as those who were forced to leave the state. However, Mask was able to defy white supremacist ideology, and—like Chesnutt's Miller—acquire the very property which once identified the white aristocracy. And in addition to subverting white-drawn property lines, Mask's ability to witness to the events of the white riot enable Chesnutt to recover the history that white supremacy attempts to deny.

In addition to the Miller/Mask connection, Chesnutt shapes a character who embodies the DuBoisian mode of the rise of "leadership of a group within a group" in his portrait of Josh Green.[103] On three occasions while both Green and Miller travel to the heart of the riot, Green asks Miller to lead.[104] After Miller refuses, Green rises to the leadership from his position at the core of the resistance movement. Chesnutt creates Green in opposition to Miller both physically and socially. In fact, he enters the novel "simultaneously with Miller's exit from the train . . . [crawling] off the trucks of the rear car." [105] In his commitment to defending against the onslaught of white hysteria, Green dutifully assumes the role of "general" in the uprising.[106] In this Chesnutt establishes Green's orientation toward collective resistance. And in his description of Josh as a martyr for the resistance in violent climax of the riot, Chesnutt subverts the image of the extrahuman black male. Using all of the prevailing images of the black type/block type, Chesnutt calls attention to Green's humanity:

> Josh Green, the tallest and biggest of them all, had not apparently been touched. Some of the crowd paused in involuntary admiration of this black giant, famed on the wharves for his strength, sweeping down upon them, a smile upon his face, his eyes lit up with a rapt expression which seemed to take him out of mortal ken. This impression was heightened by his apparent immunity from the shower of lead which less susceptible persons had continued to pour at him.
>
> . . . Like a wedge he dashed through the mob, which parted instinctively before him, and all oblivious of the rain of lead which fell around him, reached the point where Captain McBane, the bravest man in the party stood, waiting to meet him. A pistol-flame flashed in his face, but he went on, and raising his powerful right arm, buried his knife to the hilt in the heart of his enemy. When the crowd dashed forward to wreak vengeance on his dead body, they found him with a smile still upon his face.[107]

Green dies actively rejecting both white domination and African American accommodation to it. While the description of Green's death seems to be romanticized, neither his portrait nor the image of his death is shaped wholly from Chesnutt's imagination. Like Miller, Green's character is based on a historical counterpart.

Again I will turn to Thomas Clawson's description of the black response to the white riot in order to identify Green's historical counterpart.

Specifically Clawson writes about the death of the African American man who shot W. H. Mayo, the first white wounded in the fighting:

A volley tore off the top of a man's head and he fell dead about twenty steps ahead of the news-hawks. The man killed was with the negro mob which had fired . . . into whites passing Bladen Street. The shooting had caused the military to hurry to the scene. They came with the rush which marked their military precision. They later fired according to the cool order of their commander. . . . The volley which was then fired by the Light Infantry, raked the street to the east, with a hail of bullets. The result was one man killed and numbers wounded.[108]

Clawson's remembrance particularly emphasizes the brutality of the riot. One should also recognize the presence of the agentless passive in Clawson's memoir, designed to simultaneously herald white violence and to distance the violators from their acts. One of the men wounded in this attack was Josh Halsey. Halsey, however, merely provides the name for Chesnutt's character. In his portrait of Josh Green, Chesnutt commemorates the death of Dan Wright. Wright was "riddled with thirteen bullets" at the scene Clawson describes above.[109] His death two days later was, not surprisingly, reported in the *Messenger*.

The account of Rev. Bishop Strange provides another version of the volley that killed Wright. According to Strange, a white rioter wielding a pipe first knocked Wright down. He was threatened with lynching but was given another "chance":

someone said [give] him a chance . . . let him go. They did and when he had gotten about forty yards about fifty guns of all descriptions, riot guns, shot guns, and every imaginable kind of gun was turned loose on him and he was taken to the hospital where he lived two days, the Doctors said they never saw one man with as many shots as he had.[110]

What likely makes Wright's story noteworthy to the *Messenger* was the fact that he lived after the attack. Due to his survival, however short-lived, Wright would have embodied white fear of black masculinity; he would have been the kind of black type/block type character who had been used to fuel the white racialized ululation that preceded the riot. And although he was lost in the violence of the white riot, for the African American survivors of the riot he would have assuredly embodied black tenacity and militancy. In establishing Green as a martyr—and one might note that the fighting ceases after his death—Chesnutt commemorates the martyrdom of Wright, a fact that would not have been lost on contemporary black readers familiar with the details of the white riot.

Chesnutt's project remains unique because of its candor and his insistence upon righting the historical record of white riot. Chesnutt's *Marrow* not only provides a historical record of the event, it was the first novel written by an African American to receive serious critical review. And although reviews of the novel were mixed, its strength as a revisionist text resides in its potential for reshaping our views about the violence in Wilmington that the black press, given its susceptibility to fire, could not.

The *Record* was burned in order to silence the power of the African American discourse; the documentation of and commentary on events that might so "accustom" the white mind are not threatened if there is no medium through which to balance journalistic accounts of events. African American fiction is and has been from its inception a medium through which to revise this imbalance by inscribing revisions of historical "truth." In *Marrow*, Chesnutt posits an interesting relationship between history and the prevailing media of the culture through which history is inscribed. In a sense the historical record offered by the white press is a fictionalized account; the assertion in the *Dispatch* that the true results will not be printed testifies to this. However, the story of the white riot that Chesnutt presents in the novel is a part of a history that cannot be silenced, not even by fire.

3

Rioting in a State of Siege

The Cultural Contexts of Sipho Sepamla's *A Ride on the Whirlwind* and the Soweto Uprising of 1976

(A wise old man told me in Alabama: "Yeah, Ah believes in nonviolence alright. But de only way to stay nonviolen' in dis man's country is to keep a gun an' use it." Four years earlier another wise old man had told me the same thing near Pietersburg in South Africa. He said his words of wisdom in Sepedi.)

— Koerapetse Kgositsile, "Point of Departure"

You are either alive and proud or you are dead, and when you are dead, you can't care anyway. And your method of death can itself be a politicizing thing. So you die in the riots. For a hell of a lot of them, in fact, there's really nothing to lose — almost literally, given the kind of situations they come from.

— Stephen Biko, 1977

Suddenly the hundreds of tiny figures below were running, many pausing momentarily to scoop up stones and other missiles.

"Is that a police charge?" the pilot asked. But it was impossible to distinguish policemen in the melee below.

— *Rand Daily Mail*, 18 June 1976

What was happening in South Africa was known by America and Britain and the other super powers. I consider them to be. . . the same as the white people of South Africa because they did not say anything about the injustices that were happening in South Africa — until we took up arms.

— Angelina Mthenjane, 1993

Charles Chesnutt did not limit his observations about race and cultural violence to his exposé of the white riot in Wilmington, North Carolina. Years before W. E. B. DuBois wrote his theory of race, Charles Chesnutt had explored the cultural pretexts of white riot both in the United States and internationally.[1] At the time of the Wilmington *white* riot, South Africa was preparing for another, very public, kind of white violence— the first Boer War. Fought almost exclusively between the British and the Dutch, the two white "races" vying for control in South Africa, the war (as well as those which followed) paved the way, as Frank Welsh asserts, for a distinctive Afrikaner culture.[2] It was this culture that would give birth to apartheid.

Not surprisingly, Chesnutt had turned his attention to the ways in which American race praxis colored the race ideology of South African apartheid as early as 1900. In one of a series of articles Chesnutt published in the *Boston Transcript,* he focused on the crux of his theory of race: racist practice in the United States is based upon the differences white society both imagines and attributes to race. The "ethics" of white supremacy, Chesnutt suggested, allows for an association of physical, mental, and moral characteristics that shape the concept of race, forming the basis for all "color prejudice." The color line Chesnutt described, however, could be redrawn at imprecise moments, moments that were often dependent upon the desires—whether sexual, political, or economic—of the white patriarchy. Chesnutt maintained that this kind of color prejudice exists in only two places:

This [color] prejudice loses much of its importance, however, when it is borne in mind that it is almost purely local and does not exist in quite the same form anywhere else in the world, except among the Boers of South Africa, where it prevails in an even more aggravated form.[3]

It is especially fitting that Chesnutt drew this correlation well before apartheid became law in South Africa. Like many interested in the cultural legacy of race, Chesnutt recognized that American customs of "Jim Crowism" and segregation were reconstituted in the legal system of racial separatism in South Africa.

What, then, are the connections between these two cultures where white riot is always possible, especially given the fact that "race riots" occurred in nearly every decade of the modern era? There are both historical and abiding connections between these apartheid states in respect to the ways in which the black body is depicted when racial violence occurs. White privilege is reproduced through a variety of media in apartheid South Africa; in essence, black people are presented as members of a contaminating political body, one that is always available for cultural use. It is with these connections in mind that I begin to examine what happened during the Soweto Uprising of 1976. This event—one that I insist is a moment of white riot—exposes the extent of cultural similitude between these two nations.

As I suggest in chapter 1, the discourse of South African nationalism colors black South Africans in ways that force them to agitate for their social rights. The history of the antiapartheid movement in South Africa is characterized by demonstrations that are followed by increasingly violent responses from the white government. In South Africa, episodes of white riot, then, are traceable through moments of protest coming from the black community that are followed by incidents of massacre, mass imprisonment, and other forms of legal and social repression. These riots—the white and the "raced"—erupt in every decade in a cycle that is perpetuated by apartheid's insistence on white privilege. Riots are cultural events; they are what Lott calls "signifying systems" in the society.[4] This kind of cyclical violence suggests that what happened on 16 June 1976 was a part of a larger social and cultural problem. The events in Soweto, the largest of South Africa's black urban townships, were immediately described as a riot in the white press. In both the pro-apartheid and the liberal press, the riot scene was read through a series of governmental and social displacements that resist being read in any other way.

It bears repeating that the displacement of black South Africans—politically, linguistically, and physically—was a part of the prologue to the Soweto violence. In order to support white privilege in the country, the Euro-African established a system of racial separation that threatened to erase the possibility of black citizenship. In the 1970s, South Africa established independent homelands (none of which were, in fact, independent of the South African government) that were segregated according to the native language spoken by an ethnic group.[5] In reality these Bantustans provided the South African regime with the means through which to erase the possibility that anyone could be both black and a South African national.[6] And through the continuation of tribalist policies, this displacement was designed to prevent the formation of any kind of black unity. Steve Biko would describe this as the process of inscribing "Bantu-ness":

it is a subtle form of propaganda, and beyond this—teaching a kid about his Bantuness—it also teaches him to be a Xhosa, a Xhosa, who is foreign from a Zulu, foreign from a Tswana and so on, so that it entrenches in the mind of a kid the . . . unholy division of Blacks into virtual cocoons which can easily be repressed.[7]

The Bantustans not only depatronized black South Africans, but they also supported the idea that black South Africa was composed of several different, and politically divided, ethnic groups. And even as the South African government encouraged ethnic divisions between black South Africans and other "non-whites," white identity was defined as homogeneous. This feat of historical revision was as significant as the establishment of the Bantustans because white South Africans had a violent separatist history of their own. The legacies of the Anglo-Boer Wars, the marginal status of poor white South Africans, the absorption of multiple European immigrants, and the existence of two officially recognized languages were all discounted in the process of ensuring white privilege.[8]

Intrinsic to apartheid practice, then, is the ability to establish unity among "white" South Africans and division among all others, a process that should be recognizable to those familiar with American culture. In order to maintain this system of contending identities, apartheid South Africa depended upon governmental control over informational and recreational media.[9] The control of the press, publishing, and film industries in South Africa not only provided a legal means of controlling free speech, but it also provided a means of marking cultural violence as black. Through a series of suppression acts South Africa placed legal restraints on the right to publish.[10] In fact, at least five separate laws limited intellectual and publication freedom in the country, from controlling the licensing of newspapers to providing a legal means to censure individual members of the press.[11] Films, the broadcast media, newspapers, and all other written documents were also meticulously controlled. Given this history of censorship, the act of "writing" the Soweto violence was affected by the "complex" racial situation of South Africa.

KUTENI, MTA' KWETU?: SOWETO AND THE POLITICS OF WHITE RIOT

Soweto is certainly significant in the history of the resistance movement in South Africa;[12] the response of the South African government, through the actions of the South African Defense Force and the local riot police, supports this conclusion. According to Gatsha Buthelezi who, at the time of the violence was the president of KwaZulu (the Bantustan assigned to the Zulus), Soweto's importance lies in the fact that "the trauma of Soweto . . . reverberated throughout the world."[13] Still other reasons make this event intrinsic to my focus on white riot and its prologue, racialized ululation. The Soweto riot heralded a new era in the antiapartheid resistance movement not only because the black bodies at the center of the violence were unarmed black school children, but also because of the government's response to the violence. The South African government, using both the police and the defense force, turned the machinery of white supremacy against these children whom the white press characterized as "rioters." Soweto, however, was an incidence of white riot; although, given the contradictory images of the violence in the press, I am certain that this is a fact that bears further explanation.

As is true of the violence in Wilmington in 1898, the violence in Soweto in 1976 was a response to a period of white racialized ululation that erupted in white riot, an act that is rendered increasingly invisible in the modern era when governmental and police agencies initiate, rather than respond to, riot situations. Given the apartheid South African system of press censorship that could legally censure both documents and their writers, it is through the exploration of other cultural sources—literature, film, and personal narratives—what Senegalese writer and filmmaker, Ousman Sembene, refers to as the "historical memory"—that the events in Soweto are accessible.[14] In order to access the "historical memory" which frames this riot, I return to the question that opens this section: what troubled the black students of Soweto?

The violence in Soweto pitted unarmed students against the military and civil might of the South African defense force and police. Many of those who participated in the demonstration—like Hector Peterson, the first to die in the melee—were junior high school students. The now famous photograph of Peterson's limp body, accompanied by his sister in her school uniform, suggests something significant about the horrors of being defined as a dispensable black body in the path of apartheid progress. Angelina Mthenjane, one of the students involved in the melee, suggests that what happened in Soweto was not a race riot. Her narrative is worth repeating here:

I can remember very well as we were marching, we were happily singing freedom songs. Some of us were still so young that it was all fun. We really didn't know. We knew that we were demonstrating against Afrikaans, but then what? We didn't know. So, we all gathered at the stadium in Soweto and we were going to be addressed by our leaders. Before we could even know what was happening, we were confronted by the South African Army. They ordered us to disperse. We didn't see why they were threatened by our demonstration. It was just a peaceful demonstration. We were joined by the workers and other local people. So, when we didn't disperse as they wished, they started firing into the crowd. It caused a lot of chaos and havoc. People were dying and singing. All those songs. People were singing, some crying, fighting with the police. Looking at these police who didn't have that human feeling, just shooting at all of these innocent people who were without ammunition.

. . . Later, in the news after every riot, there were the usual stories that the police were being provoked beyond human endurance; that in self defense they had been compelled to open fire against the so-called rioters. The June 1976 riots as I saw them, were the bloodiest on record, even in Soweto. I have seen it happen. I could smell the tendency of death, taste of the salt of the tear gas, and rush the soldiers and stare at it with full face. Death—I have seen it on the bare face of my fellow students—but the sight of blood and the taste of death did not revolt me. Rather, the sight and smell and the firing of tear gas filled me with anger, with hatred for the police. It is something which made me understand why oppressed people go on a rampage after something happens to them. I've seen the police shooting before me in cold-blooded murder. I've seen them enjoy it, jubilant about what was done. . . .

We had no guns or anything, but they approached us and shot us with rifles and guns. They were shooting at anything that was black whether we were a part of the demonstration or not, whether we were students or not. They were just aiming at anything black . . . it was just inhumane. It was a massacre because [black] people were not rioting, basically. It started as a peaceful demonstration, but then it got much worse, you know. *They* were saying it was a riot.[15]

Mthenjane also remembers that in the aftermath of the riot, female students were the victims of sexual violence as well. Her narrative describes a white riot, one in which the violence revolved around the black bodies of these students. They were merely a part of the black body politic that was constructed as a threat to the social order. The presence of the South African Defense Force and the riot police helps to mask the white riot, shifting the public's view toward the more palatable image of a race riot.

As Mthenjane indicates, the students met to protest against the use of Afrikaans in Bantu schools. Any reading of the events in Soweto must acknowledge the ways in which the educational disparity between black and white South Africans shapes the moment. In addition to insisting that Afrikaans become the official language in black schools, the government controlled what was taught by forcing educators to teach using authorized syllabi. Prior to 1976, most of the courses in black schools were taught primarily in English. Afrikaans was not only the language of the oppressor, but it also had a limited usefulness since it is only widely spoken in South Africa. Afrikaans, then, was the medium through which South African apartheid could replicate itself perpetually. And since there was no employment available in the townships, the adult black labor traveled to white South African cities, leaving the children of Soweto to a school system that was designed to produce a black population properly submissive to white authority. Interestingly, like the racially charged political atmo-

Hector Peterson, the first victim of the violence in Soweto, 16 June 1976 (AP/Wide World Photos)

sphere of Wilmington in 1898, the events in Soweto were not without their own racial twist in that Afrikaans is not a language with a white pedigree. It developed out of the creole spoken by people of Dutch, Khoikhoi, Xhosa, French, German, and African origin; it is a part of the bastardized history of the Cape.

However, as the government attempted to use language to oppress the students, the Black Consciousness movement offered a means through which to subvert this process. Black Consciousness's insistence on black ontology provided a counter-text to the ways in which apartheid dehumanized people of color. Articulated by Steve Biko, the movement sought to rewrite the definitions of blackness in South African culture. Disseminated illegally, of course, Black Consciousness publications addressed the issues that, as Biko indicates, were relevant because of South Africa's system of race bias:

> Black Consciousness is an attitude of mind and a way of life, the most positive call to emanate from the black worker for a long time. Its essence is the realisation by the black man of the need to rally together with his brothers around the cause of their oppression—the blackness of their skin—and to operate as a group to rid themselves of the shackles that bind them to perpetual servitude.[16]

The introduction of Afrikaans into the official curriculum represented exactly the kind of shackles Biko described. The students were able to challenge the protocols of white privilege in Soweto because Black Consciousness presented them with the opportunity to envision black selfhood in ways that were radically different from the non-personhood that apartheid connected with blackness.

In attempting to redefine the possibilities for black South Africans, Soweto's students planned to demonstrate against the new Bantu educational policy. They formed the Soweto Students Representative Council, a coalition of students from all over the township. Representatives from each school met to plan a peaceful demonstration against introducing Afrikaans as a medium of instruction. The march was to be the prelude to a day of speeches and planning; however, they never reached their destination. As Mthenjane indicates, while en route to the meeting place between Phefeni Junior High School and Orlando West High School, the students were confronted by police and South African troops. After ordering the students to disperse, the police fired tear gas into the crowd and opened fire as the protesters attempted to disperse. Jack Mthenjane, who was also a part of the demonstration, suggests that Peterson's death galvanized the students:

> As I said, this was a peaceful demonstration. We were putting our case across, but when they started shooting people like Hector Peterson (as a matter of fact, he was only eleven or twelve years [old] at that time), it sparked a real anger among most of the students who were there. We started getting mad. We were rebellious, too. We wanted to defend ourselves. At the same time the forces were picking up on us, coming up fully against us with guns and dogs—everything they could come across

with—to try and suppress us as they were used to suppressing the feelings of the black people of South Africa. Basically, in that period from June 16th to the 18th, well over two thousand people were killed indiscriminately in Soweto because the government was trying to suppress the whole issue. They realized that this was one breakthrough that they could not stop and once the other force—the exiled forces— were to take part in this situation, it was going to be uncontrollable. So, the only way was to go ahead, to go all out and kill in order to try and suppress the feelings of the black population in South Africa.

Some of the reports [from the newspapers] were very sketchy. They don't tell you that two thousand were dead because they were afraid that this would spark more unrest. So, they end up saying, "Oh, five hundred are wounded and the rest are not in serious condition." As a matter of fact, we came to realize that those who were not "in serious condition" were dead. That is how we started learning how the system operates in South Africa.[17]

This narrative is worth repeating at length given the ways in which it characterizes the initial violence and its aftermath. In the three days following 16 June, students answered gunfire with stones; and in the aftermath, they burned the South African government in effigy by targeting government buildings, public transportation buses, and bottle (liquor) stores. The students' reaction sparked protests all over the country, involving South Africans in every racial category. What began as a peaceful demonstration changed in response to the white riot.

As I posit in chapter 1, white riot arises from racialized ululation, an outpouring of emotions designed to expose whatever threatens white supremacy. Given this fact, what kind of black types—perhaps reminiscent of the characterization of black people in Wilmington a century earlier— dominated newspapers images of the South African black body politic? What journalistic images replaced the face of blackness for South Africa prior to the violence? Since racialized ululation finds its outlet most often through the press, I turn to answer these questions by examining the racialized ululation that preceded this white riot.

All of the newspapers in apartheid South Africa were, of course, white owned. As I have already suggested each was operating under the legal restrictions imposed by the government. Different newspapers existed to serve all of the racial groups in the country. There were "black" papers that, while white owned, wrote with the African reader in mind. The editors, reporters, and photographers of such papers were likely to be black South Africans who were familiar enough with apartheid politics to write from the "black" perspective and still be publishable under South African press law. Among papers geared toward a white audience, there were, of course, conservative papers that embraced the spirit of apartheid, as well as papers that reflected the "liberal view," a position that Nadine Gordimer suggests remains politically useless.[18]

In reporting what happened in Soweto, these newspapers, of course, present radically different views of the event. The conservative press, quite predictably, characterizes the events as an uprising, which is just another name for a race riot since all uprisings ultimately fail. In a clear indication of the ways in which white privilege refuses to admit the existence of a political position that mediates between black and white, the "liberal" press earned Gordimer's charge of being anachronistic—of having no definitive place in the politics of the time.[19] Like the conservative papers, liberal papers report almost exclusively on the black violence in Soweto. The black presses—unfettered by their white ownership given the black writers and photographers in their employ—present an*other* view altogether. Reading the conflicting images of the riot, I believe, is a way of reading the consequences of "race" in South Africa.

In order to find the meaning behind these images, it is essential to explore the journalistic black types that were a part of the racialized ululation that shaped this riot. I limit my analyses to the Soweto riot coverage in the *Rand Daily Mail,* a "liberal" newspaper, and in the *World,* which, although white financed and managed, was edited by black South Africans, hence its subtitle, "Our Own, Our Only Paper."[20] Percy Qoboza, the editor of the *World* at the time of the riots, was a Harvard-trained journalist who was "critical of certain activities of the Soweto Student Representative Council."[21] The *Rand Daily Mail* was then edited by Lawrence Gandar, a "liberal" in the cast of Donald Woods.[22] The ways in which these papers report the events that lead to the riot are radically different. This difference casts some light on the black types that characterized the racialized ululation preceding the violence.

The *World* coverage of the events indicates that the violence in Soweto was a part of a continuous political protest. In contrast, the *Rand Daily Mail* reports that "gang" violence, black power salutes, and unfulfilled sexual desire were the reasons Soweto exploded. In an article published the day after the violence, the *Daily Mail* attempts to place the violence in perspective by describing Soweto as part of South Africa's own "blackboard jungle" (and this association with American depictions of race (mis)relations is telling here). The article details several incidents that led to the "rioting by Soweto children."[23] In its retelling of the prelude to 16 June the *Daily Mail* ignores the possibility that Soweto was related to apartheid protest and, instead, relates the violence to the sensual and sexual appetites of both the students and their teachers. The author of the article, John

Imrie, notes: "Violence in African schools has been sparked off by dissatisfaction with food, rules, teaching, the lack of books, behavior of the mas-
ters [specifically drunkenness] and even girl pupils refusing to make love to
the schoolboys." [24] The fact is that the liberal press relies on the provocative association of blackness with sexuality and consumption to explain
the "riot." Buried in the pages of the descriptions about the riot are the
markings of racialized ululation that prefigure white riot.

Accompanying the sexualized image of black students in the black types
preceding the violence are references to the ways in which blackness endan-
gers the purity of white womanhood. As was true of Wilmington, South
Africa's image of white womanhood is central to the liberal press coverage of the violence. Significantly, on the day of the riot the morning final
edition of the *Daily Mail* does not mention the tensions that erupted in
violence in Soweto. Instead, the page centers the readers' attention on a
blond woman, the size of which overshadows the page. What this image
represents becomes clear in the context of the statement delivered to parlia-
ment by Jimmy Kruger, then the minister of justice and the police. Amidst
his report on the "rowdy procession" of students who "screamed inciting slogans" and "carried banners" Kruger noted that the "vehicles of four
White women who work in the area were badly damaged. The women
were injured and admitted to the hospital." [25] The familiar use of the ways
in which the black body politic contaminates white female sexual purity
shapes the portrait of the riot in the liberal press. In fact, the paper does not
connect apartheid policy to the violence until the international coverage of
the violence does so.

As Parenti notes, the hegemonic press is self-censuring in its commitment to support the empowered.[26] And just as the prelude to the riot is
racially marked in the liberal press, the riot itself is also variously constructed around the idea of race. The *Daily Mail*'s coverage of the Soweto
violence occurs in the 17 June edition of the paper. "Riots Rage—Army
on Standby" describes "roving bands of vandals" who "burnt government
buildings, looted bottle stores, and threatened to lay siege to police sta-
tions." [27] Each of the articles concerning the violence is attributed to a staff
reporter rather than to an individual writer, except the article that refers to
the death of a white man, Dr. Melville Leonard Edelstein, the chief welfare
officer for the West Rand Bantu Administration Board. The title, "Victim
'Loved Africans,'" [28] is as much a part of the racialized ululation as is the
slant of the other articles.[29]

Rioting, according to its denotative definition, is uncontrolled and unre-
strained. However, the targets of the violence, even as they are described in

the liberal press, imply that the "rioters" specifically focused on buildings and businesses that represented the government. Throughout its coverage of the violence in Soweto, the *Daily Mail* while only subtlety indicting the police condemns the actions of the students. There are some notable differences between the *Daily Mail* coverage of the violence and that of other papers directed at a white audience, however. According to Vic Alhadeff, the first reference to the violence in the white press appears in the *Argus*. The paper sums up the violence in one paragraph that is placed "near the foot of the front page and dwarfed by two photographs of bald-headed Joe Frazier being floored by American boxer George Foreman in New York."[30] The placement of the article figures the violence as unimportant especially given the fact that it appears beneath the photograph. The photograph, however, is what speaks volumes about the events in Soweto. It reminds readers of the association with blacks and violence, especially "black on black" violence, by playing off of the battling, black bodies of Frazier and Foreman.

In some ways the *Daily Mail* is able to subvert the overtly racist coverage of the event, but only after the violence proved to be newsworthy outside of South Africa, especially in the United States. As the article entitled "Riot at Soweto" finally admits, the violence was the result of a "long felt antagonism." The anonymous writer makes it clear that police, themselves, were the rioters:

The shots that were fired by the police will reverberate round the world. There is a peculiar horror about policemen opening fire on school pupils, no matter the provocation, as America discovered at Kent State. This horror is intensified, not diminished, by the dreadful *retaliation* meted out to Whites. Our deepest sympathy goes to all the victims.[31] (emphasis mine)

Although trapped in the anachronism of "liberalism," this article is the beginning of the *Daily Mail*'s attempt to break out of its liberal mold. The association of the violence with Kent State clearly connects South African and American apartheid, and more significantly, white riot and the police and soldiers who engage in it. It is also clear that the violence that followed the white riot, the Soweto Uprising, is condemned while the actions of the white rioters are the result of "provocation."

Coverage of the violence in the *World* centers on the issues that the international press recognizes as the driving force behind the student protest: the use of Afrikaans as a medium of instruction, the inadequacies of Bantu education as a whole, the displacement of black South Africans due to the establishment of "independent homelands," and the overall oppression of apartheid. The paper had begun to focus on the impact of these policies as early as March. And by 3 June the *World* had already indicated that "race war" was possible.[32] These distinctions characterize the contrasting images of the black body leading up to and during the violence. As we have seen in the racialized ululation that marks the violence in Wilmington, the linguistic markers of race color the portraits of the prelude to the Soweto "riots."

The *World* shows the culpability of the South African government in the events of 16 June in several articles, including one that appeared in the extra edition of the paper on the day of the riot. The fact that the *World*'s reporters actually witnessed the violence as it unfolded is a key point. The coverage opens with an estimate of the lives lost; however, the lead article addresses police agency both in its title, "Police Clash with Protest Marchers," and in its tone:

> At least four people are reported dead and 14 injured in Soweto today when police clashed with some 10,000 schoolkids who marched through the streets of the townships, protesting against being taught certain subjects in Afrikaans.
>   One of the dead is a student and another an old man, who died from a stray bullet.[33]

Significantly, this article also focuses on the agency of the police officers in the violence. The fact that Hector Peterson was shot by the police is known only because of the presence of black reporters and photographers at the scene.[34] The article also notes that the "old man," the Afrikaner who "loved Africans" and whom the *Daily Mail* identified as a victim of black violence, was actually a victim of the white riot. After all, according to all of the press accounts and eyewitness narratives of the event, the police were the only rioters who carried guns into the melee on 16 June. According to the article and the photographs published in the *World*, the police who rioted at Soweto were "members of the South African Police . . . new Anti-Urban Terrorism Unit, dressed in camouflage uniform and carrying riot guns."[35] Having been prepared to combat the "terrorism" of any kind of challenge to apartheid, the police action is grounded in the ideology of white privilege that apartheid policies existed to protect.

In fact, the existence of the terrorism squad attached to an urban police department presages the characterization of the students as enemies of the state. In essence, the childhoods of the students both literally and figuratively end at the point at which they become dangerous black bodies created by apartheid. At the same time, the police action is read with the kind of nobility that the white supremacists ascribed to themselves in Wilmington in 1898. The police action, then, is sanitized. The hallucinatory shifts of racialized ululation make the white riot invisible. And since any newspaper that challenged the social situation in South Africa could be censured (as the *World* and its successor, the *Sowetan,* eventually were), fiction and film become the means by which to make white riot visible.

REENACTING WHITE RIOT: SIPHO SEPAMLA'S
A RIDE ON THE WHIRLWIND

To understand how Soweto becomes figured in other representations of the event, I will analyze Sipho Sepamla's novel, *A Ride on the Whirlwind,* as a revised history of the racial violence that began on 16 June 1976, which is a significant moment in the antiapartheid movement. Just as Charles Chesnutt captures the riot event in *The Marrow of Tradition,* Sepamla recasts the prevailing image of the Soweto Uprising. The novel provides a means to remember the ways in which Soweto marks a turning point in the struggle against apartheid. And because he focuses on the story that was not told in the liberal press and eventually silenced when the black presses were banned, Sepamla makes the white riot in Soweto visible. Further, he is able to accurately chronicle the racial violence that the white riot engenders.

The significance of using fictional narrative as a medium of protest, translation, and transformation is the message of Sipho Sepamla's *A Ride on the Whirlwind.*[36] Because Sepamla analyzes the events that engender the violence, he is able to detail the fact that Soweto was the turning point in the resistance against apartheid. In addition, as I outline later in the discussion, the censorship record of the novel also makes it relevant in terms of how language manipulated by the government misconstrues Sepamla's version of "tru-truth," a term which Sepamla signifies upon by using it to signify a truth beyond the official version of events.[37] Through his reconstruction of the intersections between apartheid, black protest, and African oral tradition, Sepamla portrays the government's insistence on manipulating truth in the politics of apartheid and its evolutionary spawn, Soweto's white riot.

A Ride on the Whirlwind opens with the "same" train that witnesses apartheid practice in *The Marrow of Tradition.* Mzi, whose name literally means *home,* is returning to South Africa in order to use the uprising in Soweto as a cover for his mission: to kill the black police officer who comes to represent white oppression in the township. In the novel, the train sequences situate references to the uprising, which at the time of Mzi's return has been raging for two days. The train represents the depth of the oppression imposed on black South Africans by the system of apartheid.

Hence, Sepamla notes that the trains come from every black township. In this the novel's opening scene, Sepamla uses the train sequence to establish the impact of apartheid on black South Africans. The train sequences also allow him to focus on the manner in which social inequality is constructed in apartheid South Africa, contrasting the black bodies of the townships against the white industrial body that is South Africa:

> The train rumbled, the passengers grumbled. What they said was not audible as the train rolled and swayed amidst the clattering of its wheels. In the course of the journey Mzi tried several things: his mind would pick on an item such as the sight of new factories along the railway line, debate the age of each factory and then give up the exercise. Sometimes he pondered over the filling up of spaces he knew to have been empty. A new station was Industrial. These were some of the little items to liven up what might otherwise have been a dull and routine trip. The train came to a stop at New Canada station. Several people leaped out of the train, others jostled to sit down on the wooden benches. New Canada was a junction station. The rail line forked out into two from this station as it entered the sprawling city of Soweto.[38]

The sights along the rail line illuminate the spread of white economic power. It is an economic growth that is dependent upon black servitude. Sepamla shapes Mzi's view of the scene by contrasting the images of white oppression outside of the train with the voiceless mass inside of it. In this manner, Sepamla politicizes the novel by focusing on the visible evidence of apartheid's impact on the black community. In addition to focusing on the familial and spiritual effects in *A Ride on the Whirlwind*, Sepamla articulates the place of the Soweto Uprising in the resistance movement. And perhaps most important, he portrays the multiracial composition of both the resistance and the apartheid communities.

In the novel Sepamla foregrounds Soweto's historical significance by using conventions of black South African orality, particularly the praise poem, traditionally called the *izibongo* or *lithoko,* in his descriptions of both the events and his fictional student leader, Mandla. *Izibongo* or *lithoko* is the oral poetic genre traditionally used to depict heroism and historic events. In fact, Mzamane describes it as the "highest form of poetic expression known to blacks."[39] Sepamla's portrait of Mandla reflects the *izibongo* form. Mandla, or more precisely the communal ethic he represents, becomes the hero of the resistance movement. Sepamla's use of the *izibongo* form situates the historical significance of the student movement.

Mandla becomes the hero in Sepamla's *izibongo,* which as Mzamane notes turns on "heroic actions."[40] As such, Sis Ida, who opens her home to the students, holds him as "more than the sum total of the number of boys and girls staying with her."[41] The police center their actions on his capture, making him the agent in every act of violence committed by Mzi. The people come to see him as the "boy which made the whitemen so scared" and turn to *izibongo* to give voice to his worth:

> Then the minds of the people paged back. No-one in living memory had received the sort of attention accorded to Mandla. Not one of the men on Robben Island was a star at Mandla's age. The veneration given Mandla began to acquire mystic qualities: some said he was the reincarnation of Tshaka and Moshoeshoe, others said he was the prophet Ntsikana. Ageing men bestowed on him the mantle of Mandela. They said it openly, that he was the son of Mandela: they saw in his face the face of that great son of the soil. His spirit began to sweep round the country as all youths worshipped his image. The faint-hearted among men found their spirits bolstered by the word Mandla. He was indeed a legend in his lifetime.[42]

For Sepamla, Mandla—whose very name means power—embodies the antiapartheid movement by involving every segment of Soweto society—male and female, old and young—who challenge the cultural assumptions that made their shared oppression possible. Responding to the ways in which the people of Soweto sheltered Tietsi Mashinini, the leader of the student coalition in Soweto, Sepamla portrays Mandla in the embrace of his fictionalized township.[43] By constructing his novel in this tradition, Sepamla establishes the meaning of the uprising in the collective consciousness of the community, using the orality of the culture to focus on Soweto's place in the resistance movement. In the words of workers, communists, and even the politically inactive members of the fictional community, Sepamla figures the uprising in terms of its place in the history of apartheid resistance. Thus, Sepamla presents Papa Duz, who "was his own history . . . a former member of the banned Communist Party," depicting the uprising in terms of both the history of the movement and its past leaders:

> "You boys bring back the good old days—the miners' strike of the late '40's, the May Day riots along the Reef and the big coastal towns. In your deeds I see walking upright once more Mandela and Sisulu, Govan Mbeki, Clement Kadalie and all the great sons of our fatherland. Your cry of Power! Power! reminds me of the resounding echoes of Mayibuye! Mayibuye! heard in Freedom Square, Sophiatown. My God!"[44]

This characterization of the movement as being both new and contiguous, both religious and cultural, is also voiced by other members of the community.

Significantly, the students' response to the white riot in Soweto, the actual "uprising," is one in which gender difference has no place. In his rendering of the students who personify the protest, Sepamla signifies on the importance of women in the movement by creating Bongi, who connects the fictional text with the historical text of the events in Soweto 1976. In the midst of a disagreement in which some of the would-be male leaders malign Mandla and other groups in the movement, Bongi is able to articulate the ways in which the movement depends upon commitment from every part of the community:

"Oh ya," said Roy as if waking from a reverie. He continued: "Mandla is losing out to Uncle Ribs."
"Uncle Ribs is a sell-out!" declared Keke. He watched the room for reaction.
"Rubbish!" cried Bongi.
"I didn't say so," explained Roy. "I asked why he wants to use us."
"He's waited till now. Why?"
"We didn't have a face. The blood of Hector, the blood of Ndlovu, the blood of many other black brothers and sisters lying there in the cold tarred and dusty streets, they gave us a face." The soft brown flesh on Bongi's face wrinkled as she said all this.[45]

By interweaving the history of 16 June with the fictional rendering of the event, and particularly by evoking the name of Hector Peterson, Sepamla situates Bongi as an eyewitness to Soweto's white riot. It is noteworthy that Sepamla makes this historical connection through the voice of a female character since the narratives of apartheid resistance, both in South Africa and America, tend to subsume the role of women in political struggles by depicting women's activism as both insignificant and extraordinary. Significantly, Bongi—whose breasts receive ample as well as critical attention in the novel—is not Sepamla's sole attempt to gender the face of the movement.

Through his depiction of Sis Ida, the most developed female character in the novel, Sepamla enacts the differences in class, race, and society that anchor apartheid culture. Through Sis Ida, Sepamla critiques apartheid South Africa's definition of blackness by describing the contending histories of her life. In fact, it is in his portrait of Sis Ida that Sepamla constructs the truth—what he describes in the words of one of the police interrogators as the "tru-truth"—of South African culture, a fact that, as I shall delineate further, is at the core of his exposé of Soweto's white riot. Sis Ida has been trained to teach; yet she shuns the classroom. Sepamla balances Sis Ida's discomfort with the classroom, a reference to the miseducation on which apartheid is maintained, by portraying the comforts she provides for the students involved in the riots. Her life, like the "riots" the author describes by inserting various news headlines in the narrative, is both shaped and narrated by the students' critique of the cultural calamities enacted by apartheid. More important however, Sepamla positions Sis Ida as the person who has the authority to reeducate those who embrace the racial hallucinations that stand for truth in apartheid culture.

Sepamla perspicaciously discusses these various "truths" through the dialogue in one of the many interrogations Sis Ida endures at the pleasure of the security police. During the initial interrogation after her arrest, Sepamla describes Sis Ida's posture as "upright" with her "hands at her back."[46] Having assumed this teaching stance, Sis Ida contradicts the expectations of her interrogator, Colonel Kleinwater. She uses the traditional name for her city of birth, Fitas, refusing to state its Afrikaner name until Kleinwater presses her to do so. She contradicts his assumption that only a "Jewish liberal" would allow her family to live together by insisting that her mother's employer is Afrikaner.[47] In the midst of telling her life's story, Sis Ida evokes an emotional response from Kleinwater when she recalls that Sophiatown, a thriving black city which was bulldozed to build one of South Africa's first all-white towns, was the place where she received her primary education. Her experiences in Sophiatown, the space where she likely underwent her initiation into apartheid, comprise an oral history that Sepamla suggests has been too long displaced by the "truth" of apartheid. Indeed at every opportunity, Sepamla portrays Sis Ida's repudiation of the racial "truths" of apartheid while she is being interrogated, subverting Kleinwater's cultural power in the exchange. In his layering of history and orality with the fictions and "truths" of apartheid, Sepamla re-creates the collective response to the white riot.

The novel also focuses on a community that is multiracial in its focus, including characters who are ideologically off balance, colorized by their social place in the society. In Noah Witbaatjie, a black man who passes as coloured by assuming an Afrikaner name, Sepamla explores the ideology of the informants who undermine the revolutionary actions of the community. In this characterization, naming becomes as important as the nature of the character. Noah, unlike his biblical namesake, jumps the revolutionary ship by Afrikaanizing his last name which translates as "white blanket." Covered in his white blanket, attempting to mask his ethnicity, Witbaatjie raves in "several languages," speaking "English, Afrikaans, Tsotsitaal, Zulu, Tswana, the lot."[48] The multiplicity of his discourses is symbolic of his place outside of the struggle, rather than a recognition of his multicultural identity. Sepamla heightens his decenteredness in his conflation of being a traitor with saying prayers in the following scene as his lover attempts to determine what he is doing:

"Reaction to . . . Mopeli High School not bad . . . believe . . . burning . . . students . . . themselves . . ."

Matlakla nearly clicked her tongue with frustration. There were words she missed. . . .

"Honey! Honey! Are you all right? Did you say something to me?" She waited for an answer with her hands cupping her breasts. The trick had always worked before. She was sure it would do so at this juncture. She waited patiently.

". . . I'm embarrassed if someone listens to what I say in prayer. I'll be joining you just now!" He waited to hear her patter away. She did. Noah dug his teeth into his lower lip and winced. The woman was getting in his hair, he told himself.

"Coming in XWEO1, Coming in."

"I read you," said a somewhat impatient voice.

. . . It was a cue for Noah to say: "Sorry for the disturbance, Meneer. Had a customer knocking on the door. And that's all for now, Meneer. Over and out." [49]

Sepamla's focus on Witbaatjie's association of prayer with his activities as an informant speaks to the character's acceptance of apartheid's privileging of whiteness as a part of divine order. Sepamla's portrait of Witbaatjie, in fact, turns on this association. In addition, his lover's body represents his embrace of the image of black women as sexual bodies available for the political manipulation of apartheid.

Witbaatjie's focus on the myth of white divinity is balanced by Sepamla's characterization of Ann Hope, a white immigrant who assists the resistance efforts. Just as he marks Witbaatjie's "racial" character, Ann is *hopelessly* marked as an outsider. Despite her use of the communal "we" in her references to the movement, Ann's whiteness makes her safe from the "bullying attitude of the police," until she smuggles Mzi out of the country at the end of the novel.[50] Her involvement, however, is based as much on her belief that she is unable to participate fully in the resistance movement as it is on her sexual attraction to the male principals in the text. She is "fascinated by Mandla" and hopes "for the day she could voice it to him without fear." [51] When Mzi seeks her help in fleeing the country, she situates herself physically as if she and Mzi are involved in a romance rather than planning his escape. Sepamla depicts this desire through both her verbal and physical cues as she and Mzi consider his situation:

Ann came back from her bedroom, perched on the divan at a point away from Mzi and said: "Well what will you have for a drink?" She put on a broad smile behind those words.

"I've got to leave!" said Mzi. His face looked hard and drawn, his brown eyes were burning with the intensity of his feelings. He was looking at Ann as if she were an enemy of long-standing.

Ann was breathless.[52]

The symbology that shapes Sepamla's portrait of Ann Hope here is tied to the threat of blackness in the apartheid state; it centers on the politicization of miscegenation as the ultimate racial threat that black men embody. Sepamla's focus on Ann's sexual response to Mzi suggests that, despite her commitment to the antiapartheid movement, she cannot escape the sexual taboo that Mzi's body represents. Her view of his body is licensed in the same ways in which the black female bodies in the midst of the 1898 Wilmington riot are regulated. Through his portrait of Ann Hope's conflation of politics and longing, Sepamla explores the way in which sexual desire provides the context for the racial dangers imagined by the apartheid state.

Tellingly, A Ride on the Whirlwind was seemingly misread by the South African Publications Control Board, which was then charged with controlling the freedom of expression in the country. The novel was banned three months after it was published with neither Sepamla nor his publishers receiving notice.[53] However, the banning was later overturned after the publisher filed an appeal. According the censor's report, the banning was revoked in part because of the inadequacies of Sepamla's audience:

> Although the likely readership of this publication cannot be regarded as sophisticated or intellectual, the likely reader would be the more arduous kind who would be prepared to labour through parts of this book . . . .
>
> The likely readership of the present novel would, as has been pointed out above, come close to a popular readership, but on the other hand, revolutionaries and potential revolutionaries find their inspiration in publications of a more direct and inciting nature. Although it presents a point of view which is contrary to that of many whites and blacks and idolizes revolutionaries, the Board's conclusion is that the book substantially amounts to a historical account of what happened in Soweto as seen through the eyes of a black contemporary.[54]

By defining the readers of the text as "unsophisticated" and "not intellectual,"—in essence, as black—the censor's report further maintains that, due to its "one-sidedness," the novel could not have an "inciting effect." [55] While it is certain that Sepamla does not attempt to incite his audience, he does not address the novel to an audience whose intellectual capacity limits its effectiveness as a protest narrative. Rather, Sepamla seeks to portray the "tru-truth" of Soweto that has been obscured by reports concerning the violence that 16 June 1976 prefigures.

What is correct about the censor's report is that fact that the novel presents a historical account of what happened in Soweto. In the novel Sepamla depicts what Mzamane suggests: that the rioters in Soweto were not the students who began a peaceful protest, ". . . but the marauding armies of police and soldiers." [56] As such, Sepamla is successful in his use of the novel to situate the historical moment that Soweto represents. Indeed, the events at the end of the novel prefigure the impending return of those who, like Mzi, will experience a "second coming," one destined to witness the return—the *mayibuye*—of the "true" South Africa.[57]

What makes the Soweto Uprising of historical importance is its relationship to both past revolutionary movements and to the resistance movement beyond Soweto 1976. Both the eyewitness narratives and the history of South Africa support the fact that Soweto marks a new phase of active—military resistance against apartheid. As Frank Molteno indicates:

> June 16, in South Africa, will never be the same again. To millions of Black South Africans, June 16 will now always be the day on which in 1976 school students in Soweto demonstrating their resistance to inferior and oppressive education were shot, gassed, beaten up, bitten by police dogs, detained . . . but fought back.[58]

Where, then, is the "tru-truth" of the Soweto Uprising? What united over 10,000 students and mobilized them to face armed police and soldiers unarmed? The answers lie in what is silenced in the press and in the sociological studies of the event, in the voices of the students themselves. Their experiences reveal that part of the history that had been silenced previously, especially during the 1980s when South Africa declared a state of emergency that allowed for the imprisonment, torture, and murder of anyone suspected of participating in the antiapartheid movement. While the Truth and Reconciliation Commission heard eyewitness accounts of the events two decades later, it is in the fictionalized accounts of Soweto that the history of the white riot is documented. Sepamla's focus on Soweto, then, is a depiction of a white riot whose invisibility is birthed in and guaranteed by the ways in which the black body is figured in the racial malformations of apartheid. Such is the "tru-truth" of Soweto.

4

Subverting the Silences

Historicizing White Riot in Fiction and Film

Statesboro, Georgia, 1904; Springfield, Ohio, 1904; Seaside, Delaware, 1906; Atlanta, Georgia, 1906; Greensburg, Indiana, 1906; Springfield, Illinois, 1908; East St. Louis, Illinois, 1917; Charleston, South Carolina, 1919; Longview, Texas, 1919; Washington, D.C., 1919; Chicago, Illinois, 1919; Knoxville, Tennessee, 1919; Longview, Texas, 1919; Omaha, Nebraska, 1919; Elaine, Arkansas, 1919; Tulsa, Oklahoma, 1921; Rosewood, Florida, 1923; Harlem, New York, 1935; Los Angeles, California, 1943; Detroit, Michigan, 1943; Athens, Georgia, 1946; Birmingham, Alabama, 1963; Los Angeles, California, 1965; Detroit, Michigan, 1967; Nashville, Tennessee, 1967; Kansas City, Kansas, 1968; Baltimore, Maryland, 1968; Orangeburg, South Carolina, 1968; Chicago, Illinois, 1968; Nashville, Tennessee, 1968; Los Angeles, California, 1992; St. Petersburg, Florida, 1996 . . .

Witsieshoek, Orange Free State, 1950; Cape Town, 1951; Kimberley, 1952; Sophiatown, 1955; Special Branch raids, 1956; Sekhulhuneland, Transvaal, 1958; Durban, 1959; Campondown, 1959; Escourt, 1959; Harding, 1959; Sharpeville, 1960; Langa, 1960; Pondoland, 1960; Cape Town, 1962; Johannesburg, 1962; Paarl, 1962; Rivonia, 1963; Cape Town, 1972; Pietermaritzburg, 1972; Carletonville, 1973; Soweto, 1976; Cape Town, 1976; Langa, 1976; Guguletu, 1976; Cape Town, 1980; Durban, 1980; Johannesburg, 1980; Elsie's River, 1980; Langa, 1985; Cape Town, 1985; Soweto, 1986; Bisho, Ciskei, 1992; Mmabatho, Bophuthatswana, 1994 . . .

The narrative structure of *A Ride on the Whirlwind* is textured by Sepamla's use of news headlines that not only reveal important information about the rising action of the novel, but that also comment on how the majority press serves the prevailing social order. The news Sepamla "reports" in the novel is always slanted toward the apartheid government, a government that considers the students' protest to be the problem with South Africa, rather than a reflection of apartheid South Africa's problem with race. And because the black press is always available for censure, it cannot counter the media's construction of the student protesters. Sepamla structures the novel around the ways in which the news destabilizes reality, ultimately allowing the prevailing system of privilege to reproduce itself.

Each of the riot episodes remembered at the opening of this chapter marks moments in which this system of white social privilege made race riots out of white riots. The preceding epigraphs, therefore, chart an abbreviated history of white riots in South Africa and the United States. Each entry marks a moment when a white riot remained largely unacknowledged while the race riot it initiated filled the public's mind with rioting black bodies, underscoring the idea of race difference in both the United States and South Africa. Even so, the race riots that ensued came as a surprise to those who did not and still do not understand the way race works in these cultural spaces. In the contemporary era, most reporters who work for majority papers—those papers that are not slanted toward a readership primarily composed of people of color—have no primary connection to the areas in which these riots occur. Living in racially and radically different worlds from the riot sites, these reporters cannot understand the pretext to riot events. As Howard Kurtz notes, the inability to engage in a discussion about race means that riot acts will always seem unpredictable despite ample evidence to the contrary.[1] The reasons that the violence in Wilmington on 9 November 1898 and in Soweto on 16 June 1976 can clearly be read as white riots is because the violence was witnessed by riot survivors who were not connected with the majority press. What happened in Wilmington and in Soweto was ultimately revealed by members of the community who intimately experienced a white riot and lived to tell about it. It should by now be clear that journalistic reproductions of events are just that; they are just as influenced by the issue of race as are American and South African cultures.

In short, the cultural power of white riot is overtly determined by images of black bodies that are never challenged by the majority press. This is the impetus behind the move to revise the histories of these riot events through fiction. As Chinua Achebe suggests, fiction enables both the writer and the audience to experience culture "directly" and "vicariously."[2] And given the ways that the genre of film allows viewers to vicariously experience a moment, both fiction and film have been used to portray riot events. My purpose in this chapter is to explore the ways in which fiction and film provide the means through which to vicariously experience the racially divergent images of white riot and race riot.

Writers of protest fiction have consistently been forced to "slip the yoke" of publication politics by producing veiled texts, texts that elicit different responses based on the cultural position of the reader. Often it is only through such masking that writers can successfully subvert the silences about racialized violence. This is especially evident given the censorship practices in apartheid South Africa, where banning, imprisonment, and exile threatened to silence the voices of these witnesses. In the United States, censorship is perfected through the politics of literary exclusion and distribution, as is evidenced in the critical erasure of Fulton's *Hanover* at the beginning of the century and in the marginalization of writers who dare to write about the complexities of race in American culture.

Although Fulton's *Hanover* included the testimony of riot witnesses, Fulton's text was successfully dismissed because African Americans could be silenced and "relegated to non-citizenship" as was declared by the white supremacy of Wilmington in the racialized political climate of Wilmington in 1898.[3] Furthermore, as this final chapter will illuminate, the silences surrounding the witnessing of racialized violence in the United States almost prevail. Despite the numerous incidents of white riot in the United States, there are relatively few renderings of riot in the literature and few eyewitness narratives survive. What I want to consider here are the ways in which such silences are broken in the visual and fictional renderings of white riot in the United States and in South Africa.

NEGOTIATING A RACIAL PEACE: THE NOVEL AND WHITE RIOT

South African apartheid literature, despite the ever-present threat of banning, has historically produced both film and narrative images of white riots. Not surprisingly, many of the writers describe their bathetic cultural position by connecting black and coloured South African cultural experience to African American experience. Black and coloured South African writers featured in the *Drum* magazine—which reached its height in the decade of the 1950s before it was banned—published stories and articles analyzing the debilitating effects of apartheid on the black body. Amidst articles and stories about black life under apartheid rule are references to the "American Negro," and the South African hunger for black African American jazz, slang, and writers, especially Langston Hughes.[4]

Beyond the *Drum* decade South African writers with international reputations explore these connections in ways that inform the popular cultural stance on apartheid. South African writers who claim white, black, and coloured identities have consistently portrayed the effects of white supremacy on a culture that invests heavily in connecting violence with the black body. Indeed, these writers quite comfortably link what it means to be "black and blue" with both South African and American apartheid. Lewis Nkosi, whose literary career began in the *Drum,* recounts an interesting discussion of race ideology he participated in while visiting a Harlem bar during his exile from South Africa, suggesting that the closeness of the two cultures is, perhaps, too close:

"This cat is from South Africa. He don't need no standard of livin'. What he needs is guns to fix them white crackers real good. Isn't that right, brother!"

When everybody had seemed somewhat mellowed in the bar I brought up the subject of the Negro in America. What were they going to do with "the white man"? Sam snorted; they all began talking all at once, shouting to be heard above the din of the juke box noise while the dainty "soul sister" sitting on the bar stool nearby peered at all of them contemptuously from under heavy eyeshades. She muttered ominously: "You niggers *talk* too much!" [5]

Writing in the tradition of South African antiapartheid literature, Nkosi recognizes the problematic silences surrounding racial violence. If merely talking too much is so transgressive in an apartheid culture, it is easy to imagine the silences that twist our understanding of white riot.

Not only have South African writers flouted the censorship practices of the apartheid era by insisting on portraying racialized violence, but they have also imbued their texts with references to specific instances of white riot. And this kind of cultural reproduction is not confined to the protest literature written by black and coloured writers. White South African writers including Alan Patton, Artol Fugard, Nadine Gordimer, Dennis Brutus, and J. M. Coetzee—to mention only a few—have also explored the protocol of white riot in the apartheid state. Coetzee's *Age of Iron,* for instance, focuses on the racial awakening of Mrs. Curren, a privileged white South African woman who faces the imminent demise of both her life, due to terminal cancer, and of her way of life, due to the cancer of racial violence that characterized South Africa's state of emergency in 1986. Significantly, Mrs. Curren is dying of breast cancer. She is Coetzee's attempt to subvert the image of *"vrou en moeder,"* the consummate wife and mother image of Afrikaner women that, as Anne McClintock rightly indicates, evolved with the Afrikaner consciousness that hinges upon "white male interests, white male aspirations, and white male politics." [6] Ultimately, Coetzee portrays Mrs. Curren as the image of apartheid metastasized; she is the white female body upon which white supremacy is authorized, moribund from the effects of its own over-production.

Not surprisingly, images of America resonate throughout the novel, which is an epistolary narrative addressed to Curren's daughter, who is living in self-imposed exile in the United States. Leaving behind the racialized ululation that shapes South African apartheid, Curren's daughter has left her mother dying along with apartheid policy in the wake of the Soweto violence. Coetzee indicates that because South Africa is not a "normal country" her daughter will not come back until apartheid has ended.[7] Yet, Coetzee's description of America reveals that she cannot escape the cultural problems she had hoped to leave behind. I quote at length here as Coetzee describes the natural and not so natural effects of living in such a culture:

> . . . I have been shuffling through the pictures you have sent from America over the years, looking at the backgrounds, at all the things that fell willy-nilly within the frame at the instant you pressed the button. In the picture you have sent of the two boys in their canoe, for instance, my eye wanders . . . to the orange life jackets they wear, like water wings of old. The dull, bland sheen of their surfaces quite hypnotizes me. Rubber or plastic or something in between: some substance coarse to the touch, tough. Why is it that this material, foreign to me, foreign perhaps to humankind, shaped, sealed, inflated, tied to the bodies of your children signifies so intensely for me the world you now live in, and why does it make my spirit sink?
> . . . The line runs out, then, in these two boys, seeds planted in the American snows, who will never drown, whose life expectancy is seventy-five and rising. Even I, who live on shores where the waters swallow grown men, where life expectancy declines every year, am having a death without illumination. What can these two poor underprivileged boys paddling about in their recreational area hope for? They will die at seventy-five or eighty-five as stupid as when they were born.[8]

Coetzee recognizes that American cultural apartheid practice is as problematic as that in South Africa. What Coetzee does here is to characterize the striking familiarity of the ritual of white racial violence in both nations. What American culture offers, then, is assuredly no better than the offerings of its South African counterpart. If American culture can only guarantee an extended life with the promise of dying ignorant of the particulars of racialized violence in the United States, it is not surprising that few non-black American writers, other than journalists, have written about white riot.

As our experiences with the majority press in Wilmington and Soweto reveal, journalists have defined race riot—that is, violence perpetrated by people embracing an identity of color—as the only kind of racialized violence in the United States. African American writers, however, have consistently connected South African and American apartheid both in the construction of the black body politic and also in the ways that this construction relates to the cultural violence of white riot. While this work provides a space to give primacy to the oral narratives of Soweto, time has made the voices of the Wilmington unrest inaccessible. What remains of these stories is in the segregated cemeteries in Wilmington. In a city that has more monuments to the confederacy than any other city in the state, the white participants in the violence are buried in the shadow of confederate monuments, resting in the midst of manicured grounds. The black victims lie in untended grounds in the neighboring cemetery, resting in the midst of ruin. While the grave markers of Alfred Waddell and Thomas Clawson speak of their nobility, the monuments to the African Americans who fell in Wilmington are rendered illegible by the overgrowth in a cemetery that, though not well maintained, is only separated from the graves of the white rioters by a shallow stream. Ultimately, while the kind of systematic legal censorship prevalent in apartheid South Africa is not a threat in the United States, this kind of cultural erasure, especially when the subject is riot, is always literally and figuratively probable.

John Hope Franklin indicates that riots replace lynching as the mechanism of race control early in the twentieth century.[9] In "The Wilmington Race Riot in 1898: Recollections and Memories," Thomas Clawson indicates that even he is aware of this shift in the manifestation of white power. After describing the details of the white rampage through the black section of Wilmington, Clawson associates the brutality used to maintain white privilege with noble violence as he describes the reasons why no lynchings occurred during the Wilmington unrest:

The night of the riot, a number of the Republican leaders of the negro race, whites, as well as several Negroes, were placed in the county jail on Princess street. Reports spread throughout the city that a crowd was organizing to break into the jail and lynch these men. Colonel Roger Moore, as the elected leader, and Captain Walter G. MacRae, another gallant confederate veteran, who later was to be chosen Sheriff of New Hanover County, determined to prevent anything which might bring eventual discredit to the community, such as a lynching party would mean. Therefore, these two leaders, quietly in the evening, shortly after dark, took their places at the jail door.[10]

Note that Clawson uses the language of white privilege in his narrative by separating the people jailed into three different categories: Negroes, whites, and Republican leaders of the negro race. In separating these "Republican leaders" from whites, Clawson has, in effect, robbed them of their racial identity, denying their whiteness because of their association with members

Alfred M. Waddell's gravesite in the shadow of the monument to the Confederate dead in the Oak Dale Cemetery, Wilmington, N.C.

of the African American community. He also carefully constructs the violence in Wilmington around blackness, erasing white participation in the riot while simultaneously compelling his reader to consider their gallantry. Not coincidentally, as incidents of riot escalate after the turn of the century, America becomes dependent upon the white riot as a means of controlling the social space.

Unlike South African literature about white riot, African American literature rarely focuses upon specific incidents of white riot. Few literary texts based upon specific white riots survive, even up to the modern period. I want to begin to examine these texts by focusing on images of riot in African American autobiography. Twenty years after the bloody riots of the 1920s, both Mary Church Terrell and Walter White wrote about specific white riots. In her autobiography, *A Colored Woman in a White World* (1940), Terrell indicates that her father was injured in an "Irish riot." What she describes is a white riot, one in which black social and political power was disrupted by racial violence. She notes:

> Shortly after the Civil War what is commonly called "the Irish Riot" occurred in Memphis. During that disturbance my father was shot in the back of his head at his place of business and left there for dead. He had been warned by friends that he was one of the colored men to be shot. They and my mother begged him not to leave his home that day. But he went to work as usual in spite of the peril he knew he faced. He would undoubtedly have been shot to death if the rioters had not believed they had finished him when he fell to the ground.[11]

Terrell refuses to further mention the riot in her autobiography, despite the fact that she indicates that her father suffered from migraine headaches regularly after the incident. Her father, a former slave, "was so fair that no one would have supposed that he had a drop of African blood in his veins." [12] Yet he was beaten in a "race riot" by rioters who had no need to question his blackness. Despite his white appearance, her father was assaulted without fear, without the need to question his apparent whiteness. He was, necessarily, victimized by people who knew him. For Terrell, then, the meaning of race is focused on the riot act, where violence is meted out based on an understanding of race that has nothing to do with the physical traces of race. Her silence is the manifestation of her coming to a disturbing understanding about race in American culture: race difference in American culture is not based upon differences in color, economics, social habits, or cultural similitude.

In his autobiography, *A Man Called White* (1948), Walter White's focus on white riot leads him to a similar cultural awakening. White, like most of the members of his family, was not visibly black. Most of White's narrative centers on the violence that he and his father encountered in the streets of Atlanta. The white riot that shaped White's childhood provides the context for his racial awakening, his understanding of what being black means in the cultural systems of American apartheid. White remembers the event as a "race riot":

Father told me as we made the rounds that ominous rumors of a race riot that night were sweeping the town. . . .

Late in the afternoon friends of my father's came to warn of more trouble that night. They told us that plans had been perfected for a mob to form on Peachtree Street to what the white people called "Darktown," three blocks or so below our house, to "clean out the niggers." There had never been a firearm in our house before that day. Father was reluctant even in those circumstances to violate the law, but he at last gave in at Mother's insistence.

We turned out the lights, as did all our neighbors. . . . There was a crash as Negroes smashed the street lamp at the corner of Houston and Piedmont Avenue down the street. In a very few minutes the vanguard of the mob, some of them bearing torches, appeared. A voice which we recognized as that of the son of the grocer with whom we had traded for many years yelled, "That's where that nigger mail carrier lives! Let's burn it down!"[13]

The White's residence, and presumably their lives, were saved by neighbors who fired at the white rioters. Certainly neither economic, social, nor color differences set the White family apart from their white neighbors. However, in the experience of the riot scene, White recognizes what it means to be black, to be "that part of history which opposed the good, the just and the enlightened" in a society shaped by the discourse of racialized violence.[14] These two narratives encapsulate the response of African American autobiography to the riot event. Surviving a white riot is the corollary to developing a race consciousness, of coming to an understanding about race in American culture.

As chapter 1 illustrates, the genesis of the Wilmington riot is a response to a white conspiracy engineered to displace black social and political power. The displacement is also clearly centered on the bodies of both black and white women who become racialized and sexualized victims of the apartheid state. In Ralph Ellison's *Invisible Man,* the riot occurs just before Invisible Man goes into hibernation at the end of the text. This rendering of riot is figured at the moment Invisible Man understands the cause of the violence. He initially believes the riot is raging because of the community's reaction to yet another dead body, that of his former partner, Clifton. However, he eventually realizes why the riot erupts; in his epiphany he recognizes that the violence has been misnamed as a "race riot." Note Ellison's description of Invisible Man's discovery of the white riot:

"We stay right here," the man said, "This thing's just starting. If it become a sho 'nough race riot I want to be here where there'll be some fighting back."

The words stuck like bullets fired close range, blasting my satisfaction to earth. It was as though the uttered word had given meaning to the night, almost as though it had created it, brought it into being in the instant his breath vibrated small against the loud, riotous air. And in defining, in giving organization to the fury, it seemed to spin me around and in my mind I was looking backward over the days since Clifton's death. . . . Could this be the answer, could this be what the committee had planned, the answer to why they'd surrendered our influence to Ras? Suddenly I heard the hoarse explosion of a shotgun, and looked past Scofield's glinting pistol to the huddled form on the roof. It was suicide, without guns it was suicide, and not even the pawnshops here had guns for sale; and yet I knew with a shattering dread that the uproar which for the moment marked primarily the crash of men against things—against stores, markets—could see it now, see it clearly and in growing magnitude. It was not suicide, but murder. The committee had planned it. And I had helped, had been a tool.[15]

Like Terrell and White, Ellison writes about an incident of racial violence that is literally orchestrated by white people that his character knew and who were protected by their privileged place in society. Invisible Man's racial awakening becomes the black community's witness of the way in which white riots are culturally constructed events. They are precursors to black-on-black violence between Ras and Invisible Man, a perfect example of how such hostility is socially engineered. The historical text of black against black political "violence"—for example, the discursive oppositions of Martin Luther King, Jr., and Malcolm X, between W. E. B. DuBois and Booker T. Washington, or Louis Farrakhan and the members of the Legislative Black Caucus—exemplifies this tension. It is significant that Ellison constructs the novel so that this event precedes Invisible Man's hibernation. Indeed, as soon as Invisible Man understands the relationship between racial violence and white privilege, he also understands that he has no place in the apartheid social structure.

Contemporary African American literature also touches on the relationship between white riots and race riots. As I indicate in chapter 1, however, representations of white riot are so persistent that they become reproduced across a range of literary forms. Significantly, African American women writers focus on the white riot/race riot relationship most. Contemporary poets are especially careful to note the ways in which riot shape the culture. Gwendolyn Brooks's poem "Riot," which sets the tone for the introduction of this work, discusses riot in terms of the how the black body is constructed in American culture. Audre Lorde also focuses on riot scenes in her poetry, principally in "Domino," "Party Time," and "Prism." The poems reflect on riot as a part of the struggle for racial, gender, and sexual rights. While there are other riot narratives that tease the racial terrain of white riot, I will attend to two contemporary writers who explore white riot: Toni Morrison and Octavia Butler. In *Jazz,* Morrison touches on the relationship between race riots and white riots in her brief exploration of the racial violence in East St. Louis in 1917. Butler also uses white riot to examine the persistency of white privilege in American culture in her novel *Kindred*.

As its title suggests, *Jazz* is a complex novel in which Morrison blends the strands of several historic events in order to capture a moment in 1926 New York City. Not only is the novel informed by the Armistice, but it also tells the story of the Great Migration, and the perturbing personal relationship between Violet Trace, her husband, Joe, and his dead lover, Dorcas. Both Violet and Joe are responsible for eighteen-year-old Dorcas's death; Joe murders her in a moment of jealous rage while Violet literally defaces her body at the funeral. It is Dorcas's memory, however, that allows the couple to reconstruct their lives. This is a critical part of the novel because in order to understand what the Traces are experiencing, Morrison makes it clear that one must understand how racial violence defines this era. Morrison shapes the Traces' lives around Dorcas's personal history because her history is shaped by a defining moment of the era: the 1917 East St. Louis riot.

The East St. Louis riot, like most riots of its ilk, has been historically documented as a race riot, although, like most of the racial incidents that are corrected in literary histories of violence, it, too, was a white riot. White rioters killed at least forty African Americans during the unrest, including a two-year-old, who, according to John Hope Franklin, was thrown into a burning building after being shot.[16] The immediate reason for the violence was the fact the a local factory had hired black workers in order to fill the demands of its government contracts, a pressing need during World War I. In *Jazz*, the riot is remembered by Alice Manfred, Dorcas's maternal aunt, as one of the events that shaped her life as well as the lives of black people in the era:

Alice thought the lowdown music (and in Illinois it was worse than here) had something to do with the silent black women and men marching down Fifth Avenue to advertise their anger over two hundred dead in East St. Louis, two of whom were her sister and brother-in-law, killed in the riots. So many whites killed the papers would not print the number.

Some said the rioters were disgruntled veterans who had fought in all-colored units, were refused the services of the YMCA, over there and over here, and came home to white violence more intense than when they enlisted and, unlike the battles they fought in Europe, stateside fighting was pitiless and totally without honor. Others said they were whites terrified by the wave of Southern Negroes flooding the towns, searching for work and places to live. A few thought about it and said how perfect was the control of workers, none of whom (like crabs in a barrel requiring no lid, no stick, not even a monitoring observation) would get out of the barrel.

Alice, however, believed she knew the truth better than everybody. Her brother-in-law was not a veteran, and he had been living in East St. Louis since before the War. Nor did he need a whiteman's job—he owned a pool hall. As a matter of fact, he wasn't even in the riot; he had no weapons, confronted nobody on the street. He was pulled off a streetcar and stomped to death, and Alice's sister had just got the news and had gone back home to try and forget the color of his entrails, when her house was torched and she burned crispy in its flame.[17]

Morrison's use of the riot in *Jazz* challenges the fact that what happened in East St. Louis was a race riot. The rioters were not "disgruntled veterans," they were "whites terrified" by the black bodies that threatened to disrupt the racial terrain.[18] Not only does Morrison imprint the novel with the Harlem silent march that protested the violence, but she also unmasks the incident as a white riot, shaping the defining moment of the novel around the dynamics that characterized race in the United States during World War I.

Like Morrison, Octavia Butler uses white riot to explore the constructions of violence and the black body in her novel *Kindred*. Butler's focus on the black body, violence, and the racial dynamics of South Africa and the United States is actually accentuated by her insistence that science fiction is a viable genre through which to revise the historical text of white riot. The novel's protagonist, Dana, is a black woman who mysteriously finds herself called back through time from Los Angeles in 1976 to Maryland in the mid-nineteenth century. In the antebellum South, Dana's body, both black and targeted, epitomizes the cultural effects of white riot in that she realizes that she can be victimized at the discretion of anyone who is white and that the legal, religious, and social institutions of the era support this possibility. Dana's journey through time is punctuated by white riot, from the mob violence perpetrated by slave patrollers—who, like the rioters described in the witness narrative of Wilmington, are both poor and white—to that perpetrated in public whippings. Interestingly, Butler inserts contemporary references to witness Dana's returns to twentieth-century "civilization." In her description of one of Dana's returns to the present, Butler inserts a telling bicentennial note about Soweto and the legacy of race in America:

> The news switched to a story about South Africa—black rioting there and dying wholesale in battle with police over the policies of the white supremacist government.
> I turned off the radio and tried to cook the meal in peace. South African whites had always struck me as people who would have been happier living in the nineteenth century, or the eighteenth. In fact, they were living in the past as far as their race relations went. They lived in ease and comfort supported by huge numbers of

blacks whom they kept in poverty and held in contempt. Tom Weylin ["master" of the plantation to which she is dragged back through time] would have been right at home.[19]

Like the two dates on the bicentennial coin, however, Dana's contemporary experience of blackness within the confines of her interracial marriage mirrors white/black gender codes of her antebellum "home." America of 1976—the same year, incidentally, that Coetzee's protagonist's daughter migrates to the States in the wake of the Soweto violence—is overdetermined by white privilege.

These novels show white riot is the single most persistent image of race (mis)relations in the last century. Home, it seems, in American and South African apartheid, is a dangerous cultural space for people of color. Literature, however, is not the primary form of experiencing the vicarious pleasures of racial violence in the twentieth century. Given this fact the discussion that follows centers on the image of riot in film, an art form that both defines this century and one that, like white riot, came of age in this century.

DO YOU SEE WHAT I SEE?: RACING RIOT
IN THE CINEMATIC TEXT

As I have suggested, there is something about the primacy of film, both the image and the genre, that is provocative. As such, film renderings of both white and race riot allow for the kind of vicarious experience that Achebe suggests is possible through literature. Both South African and American filmmakers have attempted to portray the racial dimensions of cultural violence. Films, particularly those that present a historical event through the experiences of a fictionalized character, are an effective means of making a social commentary. As a medium of protest, South African films—at least those produced prior to the 1994 all-race elections—have been largely silent about the events in Soweto because of the governmental controls that have stifled the medium.[20] South African filmmakers, though, have depicted the political dynamics of apartheid culture, as the cinemagraphic text of *Sarafina!* reveals.

Sarafina!, however, is a film based on social drama, that is, drama that originates in grassroots theater groups and public workshops. This is an important fact to consider given the use of social drama in the apartheid resistance movement, as writers and critics such as Zakes Mofokeng and Loren Kruger assert. Numerous South African dramas center on the events of 16 June marking them as a part of this movement.[21] Mbongeni Ngema, the author of both the drama and the screenplay for *Sarafina!*, is able to demonstrate that the events in Soweto arose from the racial and social ethnology of South African culture. Directed by Darrell Roodt, *Sarafina!* is the first film that he made outside of South Africa; it is also the first Roodt film involving a major Hollywood studio. The same way in which Hollywood is able to step outside of the racially charged atmosphere of the United States in its look at *Cry, the Beloved Country*, Roodt steps outside of South Africa to focus on one of the culminating events that heralded apartheid's fall. As such, in shifting from one racialized culture to another, Roodt is able to step outside of the limitations imposed on films in South Africa, while taking advantage of the American hunger for images about the racial situation in South Africa. Roodt's other films include *Jobman* (1989), *The Stick* (1987), and *A Place of Weeping* (1987), all of which comment on the "tragic paradox" of apartheid by focusing on the experiences of coloured South Africans.[22] In *Sarafina!* he contextualizes the impact of apartheid's response to the children involved in the black resistance movement that would change substantially after the racial violence in Soweto.

The film specifically analyzes the social milieu in South Africa that leads to the violence in 1976. In essence, as *Sarafina!* unfolds, the issue at the center of the protest is not the institution of Afrikaans as a medium of instruction. Rather, the film clearly demonstrates the threat that Bantu education policies embody. The students' rejection of these policies is tantamount to a conscious rejection of the social inequalities that literally define life on "the black side of the great divide."[23] Ngema and Roodt are, therefore, consciously exact in their portrayal of the reasons why Soweto erupts in 1976. *Sarafina!* is a complex merging of protest drama and documentary told through the experiences of a schoolgirl, Sarafina, "the queen of Soweto." Her story is representative of black South African childhood in that her adolescence is shaped by the impact of apartheid. Apartheid witnesses her father's death while "fighting for the Resistance," her mother's servitude as a housekeeper in a white city, and the problem with her "Bantu" education. As a child of Soweto in the 1970s, Sarafina's life centers on the two worlds of South Africa: the white privileged and the black oppressed.

From the opening scene of the film, the audience is drawn into the spectacle of a train as it carries its human cargo into the white cities at the dawn of a new day—a replication of the realities of a morning in Soweto. The train, in South African as well as African American discourse, is the only thing that can cross racial lines specifically, and, interestingly, it is also an omnipresent physical reminder of where these lines are drawn. The train literally tracks the physical racial divisions along with the concomitant social differences this division implies. As a popular folk song recounted in the film asks: "Where is this train going? / To take the fathers and mothers? / And where is this train going?" Its existence validates and reproduces white privilege each time members of the black labor force prove that they are dependent upon the very structures that oppress them. Throughout the film this image of the train is developed as a symbol of South Africa's racial troubles. The train materializes, both in the foreground and in the background, each time the characters confront interrogation, torture, and upheaval.

As the image of the dawning day in *Sarafina!* signifies, it is also a new day in the revolution in Soweto. Roodt and Ngema foreground a group of student demonstrators in this scene as they emerge from the shadow of the train on a mission to fire bomb the school. As the child-revolutionaries enter the school, the classroom is figured as a participant in their oppression. To illustrate this point, the filmmakers focus on a Molotov cocktail that provides the only light in this predawn scene, illuminating a globe that sits on the school desk beside a stack of papers. The black board is set aflame at the word "declination," representing the students' refusal of Bantu education, its authorized syllabi, and of apartheid policy itself. In this sequence the film cuts across the range of social reflections of apartheid, from the interruption of the family structure to the circumvention of the educational process, all of which can only be redressed by acknowledging the historical and linguistic constructions that created them.

What apartheid does to the family structure is evident in Sarafina's family situation, which is clearly representative of the black family in apartheid South Africa. Sarafina's mother, a domestic worker in Parktown—and, as such, a temporary alien—is as removed from Sarafina's life as her father, who died before he even had the opportunity to fight in the resistance movement. This lack of familial rootedness is further emphasized in the portraits of Sarafina's extended family. Her family is literally constructed in the dismal realities of black South Africa under apartheid: her uncle, who equates manhood with drinking beer; her argumentative aunt; and her four siblings, who look to Sarafina as a surrogate mother. And the struggle against apartheid requires active resistance which further strains the familial relationships of those involved in the struggle. Sarafina's teacher, Ms. Mazembuka, portrayed by Whoopi Goldberg, lives with the hope of starting a family despite the fact that her husband, Joe, has had to go underground because of his commitment to an antiapartheid group that embraces armed confrontation.[24] Sabela, the black police officer played by Ngema, lives alone in a "middle class" house in Soweto. As a black police officer he is the embodiment of the apartheid system, a contradiction of his right to authenticate his own existence. Through these portraits Roodt and Ngema attempt to illustrate the ways in which apartheid disrupts black family life at every social level.

In addition to portraying the familial separations that define black South Africa, *Sarafina!* also focuses on the spiritual disconnection within the people of Soweto. The indigenous religions of the region hold the ancestor as an integral part of the spiritual lives of the people who embrace traditional cultural practices. In representing the broken spirituality of the people, Ngema visualizes a culture that is disconnected from the past. There is no reference to the ancestors; however, in Ngema's mythological world the ancestor-image is linked with the resistance struggle. Rather than "grasping the tail of the ancestors," Sarafina celebrates her spiritual connection to Nelson Mandela.[25] This connection becomes a focus of the film from its beginning. Sarafina is first introduced in the film as she lights a candle to illuminate Mandela's portrait. She "prays" to Mandela about what apartheid means in her life. Her spiritual connection to him is also figured in her desire to literally embody Mandela by portraying him in the school play. It is a connection that remains intact until Sarafina's world falls apart in the aftermath of the white riot at Soweto.

The film sequences also draw attention to the disparity between the black and white worlds. Parktown, where black women sweep the streets continually, is a place in which the family is whole; however, its wholeness is dependent upon the disintegration of black family life and the displacement of black labor from Soweto. In almost every way the disintegration of familial ties in the film mirrors the situation described in the narratives of those involved in the antiapartheid movement. Beyond the focus on apartheid's effect on black family life, *Sarafina!* centers on the locus of the uprising in 1976 and on the ways in which Bantu education (that is, up until the time of the Soweto uprising) is used to support apartheid racial policy. It is in this context that the film is the most subversive. The school buildings, which on the inside appear to be as stylized as the one burned by the students in the opening scene, are actually marked by the evidence of the resistance struggle. The words "AK-47," "*Amandla*" (power), and "Ruth First" (an ANC member who insisted on the fact that military action must have a political context) appear as graffiti on the school walls and in the background of scenes revolving around the students' daily lives.[26] In these sequences Roodt draws attention to all of the options for resistance that were available to the students of Soweto: nonviolent confrontation, violent confrontation, and embracing the liberating ideology of Black Consciousness. School, then, is doubly symbolic in the film; it is both a site for anti-apartheid resistance as well as pro-apartheid indoctrination. Only one of the teachers, Goldberg's character Mazembuka, educates the students to give them a sense of black pride. Like those who defied the rules of apartheid during the resistance struggle, Mazembuka is subsequently arrested for her refusal to teach the authorized syllabus and is killed while she is in custody. Significantly, Goldberg portrays a history teacher whose revisionist stance allows the students to acknowledge the relationship between the Boer version of history and the validation of apartheid practice. It is evident that Sarafina comes to understand this manipulation given her ability to translate and to challenge the language of white violence after her own arrest. She challenges the "official" version of the death of Mazembuka who, like many of the thousands of people detained in 1976, "died of suicide." As the witness narratives reveal, suicide means murder in the language of apartheid. It is significant that when Sarafina's interrogator advises her that Mazembuka has committed suicide, she responds by saying, "You didn't have to kill her." Through her ability to translate the language attendant to white riot, Roodt and Ngema mark Sarafina's political coming of age.

The acknowledgment that the white text of apartheid must be translated, that meaning lies outside of the denotative language of the system, is one of the themes that is illuminated in witness narratives of the violence. The official language used to describe the violence and its victims skews meaning in the same way that it reorders black identity in the culture, through linguistic slippages and official usage of racialized terms. Through the use of official language, the fate of those incarcerated, tortured, and killed while in police custody is erased. As such, people who are described as "not in serious condition," as Jack Mthenjane indicates, are already dead.[27] Sarafina's ability to ascertain meaning beyond the official line is a necessary part of her political education.

Although *Sarafina!* explains the social context of the violence in Soweto, Roodt's dramatization of 16 June 1976 is limited. The brief sequence concerns the moment at which the students meet the police in a violent confrontation. The students, like those in Soweto, face guns armed with stones. The scene then shifts to focus on the police presence in the townships and the subsequent arrest and torture of Sarafina and her fellow students. The focus, then, is on the social ramifications of political action, as Ngema and Roodt concentrate on the legacy of the Soweto "Uprising." The rising action of the film—especially when the police shoot Sarafina's boyfriend,

Crocodile, in the back in the same manner that Hector Peterson was shot during the violence in Soweto—allows the viewer to vicariously experience Soweto's white riot of 16 June 1976.

Perhaps the most detailed film sequence of the riot occurs in Richard Attenborough's *Cry Freedom*, a film based on Donald Woods's *Asking for Trouble*. The film centers on how Woods is transformed from a white liberal, enjoying the privileges afforded by apartheid, to a politically aware South African in exile. Woods must leave the country so that he can publish an account of the circumstances surrounding Biko's death while in detention. The underlying motivation for Woods to publish Biko's story is the fact that he also wanted to publicize his own experience as a banned person in South Africa.[28] For Woods, the former white liberal, then, the license to denounce apartheid policy must be couched in his position as the chronicler of the circumstances surrounding Biko's death. *Cry Freedom,* though not dedicated to the Soweto violence, includes over five minutes of footage that accurately details the events of 16 June. In an extended memory sequence that occurs when Woods and his family fly over South African air space as they begin their exile in England, Attenborough chooses to reconstruct the Soweto riot. His portrait captures the student protest that forever changed South Africa by centering on the dead body of Hector Peterson as it is being carried from the scene by his classmate and sister. Attenborough signals the importance of the violence in Soweto—and of Peterson as an icon of the struggle—by juxtaposing the film version of the photograph that "told the world what was happening in South Africa" against the image of the Woods family's escape from South Africa. This scene is significant because Woods would ultimately tell the world about another South African truth: that even white South Africans are affected by apartheid policy.

Yet the implications of the white riot are not depicted in these texts because of the limited focus of each film. Neither film is a documentary about the riot itself, and neither can encapsulate what Soweto means in the history of resistance in South Africa. South African filmmakers have tenaciously depicted racial violence and the cultural mores that make it possible. However, censorship laws have controlled film content as well as distribution possibilities. Thus, films that depict South African race relations have frequently been directed to an alien audience. Not surprisingly, as Roodt's oeuvre suggests, the most frequent alien audience is found in the United States.

American filmmakers have had difficulty depicting racial violence outside of the documentary mode. Although Oscar Micheaux captured a lynching bee in *Within Our Gates* (1920), riot did not become a thematic focus of African American filmmakers until the contemporary era. Sidney Poitier's film debut, *No Way Out* (1950), merely suggests that white riot is a possibility.[29] Poitier portrays Luther Brooks, a newly licensed physician, the first black physician hired at a hospital located in a metropolis that incorporates two racialized areas: the all-white Beaver Canal and Nigger Town, whose name needs no further racial explanation. Brooks is accused of murdering one of the Biddle brothers, one of two petty criminals who were shot by police while attempting to rob a gas station. In fact, the prisoner dies while Brooks is treating him in the prison ward of the hospital. The surviving brother, whose racist stance betrays his inability to believe in even the possibility of a black doctor, witnesses his brother's death and swears that he will avenge his murder. Spurred on by the white racialized ululation that ensues, the inhabitants of Beaver Canal plan a white riot, arming themselves with whips, chains, and other weapons they find in the Beaver Canal junkyard. The film's director, Joseph Mankiewicz, actually depicts one of the principal agitators practicing for the white riot by beating and verbally debasing a heap of black metal; sadly, it is the closest that 1950s Hollywood ever comes to depicting white riot. Of course, the white riot never happens on camera. Instead, in a move that will become a technique used in the news media when white riots occur, the white riot is displaced by a race riot. Having been forewarned of the Beaver Canal plan, the men of Nigger Town attack Beaver Canal, and the race riot, complete with images of terrified white women, becomes the focus of the film. Interestingly, reminiscent of the dilemma faced by Dr. Miller in Charles Chesnutt's *The Marrow of Tradition,* Poitier's character must save the life of the surviving Biddle brother, who, despite the fact that the doctor had been proven innocent of murder, attempts to murder the good doctor at the end of the film. The American viewing public would have been prepared for this kind of racial displacement by the erasure of the white violence that occurred during the Detroit white riots and race riots of 1943.

Ultimately, the portraitures of white riots are only slightly drawn. As Donald Bogle indicates in *Toms, Coons, Mulattoes, Mammies, and Bucks,* when riot is the subject of the film text the black male body, not the construct of race, is the focus. Consider Bogle's reading of *Riot* (1969), a film starring football legend Jim Brown:

One scene in his prison drama, *Riot,* seems to have been inserted not only to shock the sensibilities of the mass audience, but also to titillate some of the homosexual patrons. In the film Brown is approached by a white prisoner who begs to spend the night with him. As Brown's character remains aloof and implausibly untouched, the homosexual's passion merely grows.[30]

Riot scene from *No Way Out* (1950) (Museum of Modern Art Film Stills Archive, New York)

Made in the wake of the Watts riot of 1965, the title of the film surely depended upon the audience's association of it with these riots, which at that time were the costliest riots in the history of the country. And—given the manner in which black male bodies are constructed prior to white riots— the superhuman, supersexual aura constructed around Jim Brown's body indicates that the white racialized ululation was at its height, calling for the need for further violence. The racial violence of the 1960s in Detroit, Kansas City, Baltimore, Orangeburg, and Chicago, then, exemplify the violently generative power of racialized ululation in American culture.

Interestingly, until Spike Lee depicts riot in *Do the Right Thing* (1989), representations of riot in African American film focused on the social forces that prefigure riot, rather than upon white riot itself. Through the social and cultural dynamics of the riot scene, Lee dramatizes issues of class, ethnicity, and race relations in New York. Significantly, these are the same issues that resurface in the Los Angeles Rebellion in 1992. In *Do the Right Thing*, riot is again figured around the black male body, that of Radio Raheem, who is killed by the police in the midst of a white riot. One of the ways that Lee characterizes riot, then, is by signifying on the cultural gaze affixed on black bodies and most particularly on black male bodies.

White rioters pursuing a black man across Woodward Avenue in Detroit during the rioting on 21 June 1943 (AP/Wide World Photos)

In his portrait of white riot, Lee foregrounds the culture of consumption that surrounds the black male body. Significantly, the riot is grounded in a protest mounted by Buggin' Out, a young man whose "blackness" is simultaneously marked by his Afrocentric hairstyle and erased by his conspicuous consumption of Eurocentric products, ranging from his sneakers to his insatiable desire for Sal's "finest" pizza. When Lee portrays Buggin' Out's protest about the lack of blacks featured on Sal's Italian "wall of fame," the scene is filled with black men who are conspicuous consumers, despite the fact that they are themselves in danger of being consumed by Sal's version of the American dream. Lee suggests this repeatedly in the film by constantly framing scenes in which Buggin' Out and Mookie, who is portrayed by Lee, are pictured under the sign that advertises Sal's pizzeria. These images are mirrored in the shop's window where they not only advertise the wares of the pizzeria, but also represent the cultural shadow of consumption that is directed upon the bodies of black men. In essence they suggest something significant about the ways in which the black male body informs the riot scene in *Do the Right Thing*.

Radio Raheem, the consummate superhuman black male, literally fills the cinemagraphic frame in such a way that he even "walks in stereo."[31] Mookie, for instance, is the only non-white male on the other side of the racial divide prior to the point at which the race riot erupts. Finally aware that he is the antihero in this scene, Mookie seemingly starts the riot by throwing a trash can through the pizzeria window. While this is an interesting interpretation of the riot in the film, it is essential to understand that this riot sequence is not the only one depicted in *Do the Right Thing*. Lee does an exceptional job of detailing the ways in which the black body becomes imaged in apartheid culture. For those viewers who are susceptible to the displacements of apartheid culture, black people are merely types; they become defined by what their black bodies represent, rather than by their individual subjectivity.

In addition to portraying the objectification of black men in the film, Lee also constructs black women as sexual abstractions. From the opening sequence of the film, Lee focuses on the body of Rosie Perez, alternating between depicting her in positions of radical protest and sexual performance. And Sal's desire for Mookie's sister, Jade, is placed immediately before the onset of the violence. Accordingly, what we see in *Do the Right Thing* are black female bodies that are hypersexualized; black male bodies that are superannuated with power; and a black community in which the only means of economic production is controlled by an Italian family that is still in the process of constructing its own whiteness. At the moment all of these images coalesce, the scene is set for the white riot that claims the life of Radio Raheem, one that is, of course, displaced by the race riot that follows.

As is true of the renderings of race riot in American culture, the riot the American viewing audience recognizes is the one in which black bodies fill up the violent space. The disavowal of the white riot which precipitated the violence is suggested in Lee's depiction of the "race rioters." Most of the rioters are anonymous figures, extras in the scene. In fact, the only recognizable character participating in the retaliatory riot is Smiley, a stuttering near mute who, significantly, rarely smiles. Yet these familiar images belie the fact that there is a white riot depicted in the film. In fact, the violence that begins inside of Sal's Famous Pizzeria mirrors scenes of white cultural violence in the apartheid state. Note that prior to what Lee describes as a fight that takes place inside of the restaurant, Sal confronts Radio Raheem, Smiley, and Buggin' Out, not as people, but as black bodies threatening to reconfigure the power relationships that maintain his microcosmic culture. The significance of this point is heightened by Lee's portrait of Sal as a man who, despite a veneer of liberalism, is always on the verge of violence. In fact Sal's opening remarks end with his assertion that he is "going to have to kill someone today," and his bat is always at the ready. Moreover, the racialized ululation that precipitates every incident of white riot is implicit in the racism which Sal's son, Pino, spews throughout the film. Like those who embrace the idea of white supremacy, Pino is affected by the racialized ululation he embraces each time he insists that his racist attitudes are grounded in what he reads. In addition, in the moments before Sal initiates the violence by "killing" Radio Raheem's "jungle music," it is important to note that Sal no longer refers to the men by their names. Ultimately, Buggin' Out, Smiley, and Radio Raheem are black bodies; they are what Sal names them: "black cock suckers" and "niggers." [32]

Most important, echoing Soweto, the police presence on the scene signals the fact that the racialized ululation has done its cultural job. As such, the white riot culminates with the death of Radio Raheem at the hands of the police who, true to their belief in the superhumanity of the black male body, manage to believe that he is merely pretending to be dead. In the end, then, while Lee does not focus on a specific episode of white riot in *Do the Right Thing*, the image of white riot as the cultural text of America is a recognizable subtext.

Two additional films that dare to portray white riot are *Rosewood* (1996), a film based on the white riot that eradicated the black presence in Rosewood, Florida, in 1923, and *Riot* (1997), a Showtime original film concerned with the Los Angeles racial violence. The persistent production of films that depict white racial violence suggests that there is some recognition of the fact that white racial violence has continually sustained America's system of white privilege. Even for those who sincerely believe in the existence of a "race card," these novel and cinematic reenactments of white riot make it impossible to ignore the manner in which the ritual of white riot has consistently and historically used race to control the cultural space. In short, the structures that were designed to maintain white privilege form the basis for the episodes of race-based violence, which have erupted in South Africa and the United States, bringing the races intimately and violently together. Writers and filmmakers who insist upon depicting white cultural violence have created a safe space in which to disrupt these structures by making white riot visible.

Epilogue

The Tie That Binds—Los Angeles and Mmabatho,
White Riot on the Cusp of a New Millennium

The predominant portion of gross violations of human rights was
committed by the former state through its security and law-enforcement
agencies.
— *The Truth and Reconciliation Commission of South Africa Report*, 1998

[S]tudies indicate that minorities and people of color have less confidence
and trust in law enforcement than do whites. Several factors probably
contribute to the mistrust . . . [including] negative interactions between
minorities and people of color and law enforcement personnel (which may
range from unjustified police stops to improper use of force), racial
disparities in the administration of justice (including disparities in
incarceration rates, sentencing, and imposition of the death penalty), and
the lack of diversity among law enforcement personnel (for example,
police, prosecutors, and judges).
— The President's Initiative on Race Advisory Board, *One America in the 21st
Century*, 1998

As I have already noted, there is something insidious about the ways
in which apartheid culture manufactures images of racial and ethnic
identities and subsequently identifies whiteness as the antithesis of these
racial constructions. The most vilified representation is that ascribed to
blackness. Ultimately, the black body becomes a social text which can be
written upon at the pleasure of white privilege. And this is a process that
is assiduously guaranteed in the apartheid state through the ways in which
the law is enforced, assuring the alienation of people of color. This guarantee is what Foucault has in mind when he asserts that power often assumes

the "forms of peace and the State."[1] It is the black body that is the focus of white supremacist rage in Wilmington because it is only through such objectification that the American dream, dependent as it is on the notion that race difference necessarily involves a hierarchy, remains unchanged. The linguistic bastardy of apartheid also writes a text around the black bodies of Soweto. Accordingly, the Soweto riots will always be defined by the socially generated images of black bodies that are perpetually hypersexualized and riotous.

As I have tried to delineate in this book, white riot is related to the apprehension associated with potential cultural changes aligned with the passage of time. When the subject is race, the dis/ease is always figured in terms of the power relationship that is maintained by white riot. The dis/ease of racial violence at the end of the twentieth century has exacerbated the cultural tensions that have always defined these apartheid states. What, then, is the image of white riot at the cultural crossroads of the new millennium as South Africa attempts to reconfigure itself as a nonracial society and as the United States moves to embrace a notion of multiculturalism, when neither nation has quite managed to dismantle the legacy of white privilege? The answer to this question may well be found in the analyses of the cultural legacies of riots that occurred only a few years apart: the racial violence in Los Angeles in 1992 and in Mmabatho—the capitol of Bophuthatswana, one of the former South African Bantustans—in 1994.

The videotaped image of the brutal assault of Rodney King by several Los Angeles police officers was transmitted around the world on almost a daily basis from the time it initially aired on 7 March 1991. During the months following the broadcast, the videotape permeated the popular culture in the news, in music videos, and in the discourse about race, class, and ethnic relations. Following the acquittal of the officers involved in the beating just over one year later, the videotape provided the context to the text of what is popularly known as the Los Angeles Rebellion, as race once again colored the national understanding of justice.

In Mmabatho, the image of the bodies of three, bloody white men laying beside their blue Mercedes Benz also captured the attention of the international media on 11 March 1994. The men—Alwyn Walfaardt, Fanie Uys, and another identified only as Fourie—were members of the Afrikaner Volksfront, a *broederbond* dedicated to white supremacy and adamantly against the first all-race elections in the history of South Africa. They had come to Mmabatho armed with guns and apartheid intentions in order to prevent the people of the Bantustan from participating in the 1994 all-race elections; they were shot after firing upon unarmed civilians, and finally, upon members of the Bophuthatswana defense force. One of the eyewitnesses of these violent exchanges was Bob Drogin, then a reporter for the *Los Angeles Times,* who—in describing their deaths at the hands of a "black man in a green police uniform"—indicated that they were executed in cold blood. Certainly, there is a relationship between Drogin's reading of this event and the invisibility of white riot. Los Angeles and Mmabatho are the legacies of the cultural texts of apartheid consciousness. As the confessions of South Africa's *Truth and Reconciliation Commission of South Africa Report* and the United States' *One America in the 21st Century* reveal, police and political violence continued to hide white riot on the cusp of the new millennium. It is clear that what is needed is an exploration of the ways in which this legacy informs the media's—and hence, our own—assessment of these riot events.

WHITE RIOT: THE LOS ANGELES REBELLION UNMASKED

As Los Angeles cindered in the wake of the violence, members of the majority press reported not only the events but also their surprise. According to Howard Kurtz, the majority press had "trouble coming to grips with racial animosity. It is the subject everyone talks about and few write candidly about. It fascinates and frightens us at the same time." [2] The riot, however, was not a surprise to most of the black presses across the country. My discussions about the riot with members of the black press corps, including Sheryl Brown of the *Black Voice News,* confirmed what I already knew about the reactions of black readers and writers of the news. [3] For the community of the variously disempowered, the riots were not only expected but were attributable to the continuing problems relating to race that define American culture. As Rusty Cundieff suggests in his spoof on rap culture and the Los Angeles riots in his first film, *Fear of a Black Hat* (1993), the riots were a response to centuries of racial harassment. He notes:

> You know how when people mess with you and put you through a lot of shit? You know? And you feel bad and then they put you through some more shit? And, it's like, you get tired of it and you feel just like "FYM": fuck y'all motherfuckers. You know? And see, that's what the whole riot was about. The riots was one big FYM; fuck y'all motherfuckers. [4]

Ice-T, one of the rappers whom Cundieff caricatures in the film, illuminates this difference thusly, "April 29, 1992 was the happiest day of my entire life." [5] The media remembers Los Angeles as one of the times during which America was split along racial lines. These polarized responses to

the same event also inform the differences between the ways in which the
riot events were figured in the press accounts of Wilmington and Soweto.

The King beating and the court interpretations of the event never fall
outside of the normative gaze of white society. From the view of George
Holliday, the man who recorded the videotape of the King beating, to the
all-white jury that vindicated the police officers in the Simi Valley court-
room, King's body is the text that is interpreted through the eyes of white
society. In this work I have tried to problematize what happens when these
interpretations replace black identity, making the black body part of the
text of apartheid. The videotaped beating of Rodney King is such a text.

When Holliday—as an amateur videographer—aimed his new camera
at the street and videotaped the King beating, he noted that he was "barely
aware of what was unfolding as he filmed it."[6] In fact, Holliday admitted to
watching only part of the scene. However, other witnesses to the event, also
residents of the Mountainback Apartments in which Holliday lived, were
horrified by the scene.[7] Yet although Holliday was portrayed by the media
as being sensitive to the brutality of the event he chronicled, he was not
immediately aware of what he had observed. Holliday was literally unable
to see King—the epitome of the superhumanity that characterizes white
apprehension of black males—as a victim. What I am suggesting is that
Holliday's inability to witness this event is a part of the cultural phenomenon surrounding the black body, particularly given the composition of the
other the images he videotaped, that segment of the tape that was never
aired during the year in which the videotape was likely the most watched
in history.

The popular discourse about the King videotape portrays Holliday as
the owner of a new camera who simply wanted to try it out. However, at
some point, Holliday, as videographer, decided what he wanted to record
with his new video camera. His decisions, of course, were unavoidably
based on the sensibilities of his cultural orientation. What informed his
decision is what Stuart Hall and Paddy Whannel describe as the "modi-
fying effect" that the media has on the "imaginative experiences" of the
viewer.[8] Holliday necessarily figures King within the imaginative experience of the racialized lens of American society. What was not shown in the
broadcasts points to how Holliday imagines the black male body in this
context:

Holliday, who manages a plumbing business in North Hollywood, had been taping
just about anything to practice using his SONY Handicam—"a cat licking its paw,"
he said, giving one example. The same tape depicting the beating of Rodney Glenn

King of Altadena includes footage Holliday shot at a neighborhood bar where Arnold Schwarzenegger has been filming "Terminator II." [9]

As a series of images, the cat, King, and Schwarzenegger beg to be interpreted. Given what happens to black people in a culture maintained by white riot, the juxtaposition of these images confirm that Holliday's imaginative experience is limited when the body in the video frame is black.

Certainly, the beating is somehow aligned with entertainment, especially the genre of entertainment for which Schwarzenegger is known. Aside from the films produced during the "Blackploitation" era of the 1970s, characters of color have usually provided the bodies for the body counts that typically inform not only action films but horror and suspense films as well. Given the presence of the other images on the videotape, King is the image of the dispossessed, caught someplace between object and entertainment. Imagined between these images, King's body seems to be a point of cultural reference. As such, the focus of the pre-riot discourse is marked not only by references to the beating but also by the repeated broadcasts of the videotape. After selling the videotape for five hundred dollars, Holiday attempted to recuperate his financial loss after the videotape was popularized by the various news and informational media. In keeping with the culture of consumption as it relates to the black male, the videotaped image had a market value that increased exponentially each time it was shown.

Holliday's video also reveals something significant about the manner in which the American public came to view King as a social body. The videotape details the assault while motorists pass, apparently oblivious to the brutality of the scene. Slowing only to participate in the normative gaze, the motorists focus on the black body—an object usually associated with violence—rather than on the violent scene they witnessed. The fact that the beating was compelling enough that the traffic slowed to watch suggests that the passersby were not desensitized by the violence. Rather, as members of a cultural audience the motorists—regardless of their racial backgrounds—were able to accept the brutality as normal response to King's blackness. King's identity, both African American and male, characterizes the brutality in ways similar to the emotions surrounding a lynching. The motorists are a part of a cultural audience that is desensitized to white racial violence, especially when the victim of the violence is black. They witness a white riot, as vivid as those that occurred in Wilmington and Soweto, a century and a few decades apart, but remain comfortably unmoved by the violence of the scene.

History seemingly repeats itself when the attorneys for the police rioters in the state trial were able to prove the innocence of their clients because they knew that the all-white jury in Simi Valley (despite the pronunciation of the first name of the city) would not be able to see the white riot. The members of the jury could not even determine that King had sustained any injuries, their blindness uncomfortably reminiscent of the witnesses to the Pana incident (see chapter 2) when the press reported that witnesses could not ascertain the effect of a five-hundred-volley Gatling gun assault on a black male body. Stacey Koon, the ranking officer present at the beating, was one of the two officers who was found guilty in the federal trial. Writing in *Presumed Guilty,* Koon is also illiterate when the black male body is the text:

King was knocked to the ground, doing a one-point landing, face first, into the asphalt. This was the second time his face had been roughly introduced to the pavement, and most of us at the scene believed this is when the cheekbone was fractured.

But, incredibly, again, Rodney King rebounded as if he hadn't been touched. He was back up on his knees, trying to rise again, and Powell continued to strike him in the arms, hoping to take out King's support so he'd fall back to the ground. . . .

I believed that King . . . was an extraordinarily dangerous suspect.[10]

In both instances, the social figuration of the black male ultimately discounts his humanity while simultaneously portraying him as superhuman. The focus on King's body leads to the events in Los Angeles 1992, the most horrific and costly racial violence to date. And true to the media's need to portray racial violence as black, the Los Angeles unrest is always remembered with the black bodies present in the race riot that followed, rather than as a consequence of the white riot that forever changed the life of Rodney King.

These two riots, the one white and the other portrayed as black, also turn on the association of black male sexuality with the necessity of white racial violence. It is because of this association that Koon facilely describes King as being sexually aggressive, moments before the beating begins. Koon notes that:

Melanie Singer decided her command presence was required. She shouted at King to show her his hands [King was already on the ground]. Recognizing the voice as female, King grinned and turned his back to Melanie Singer. Then he grabbed his butt with both hands and began to gyrate his hips in a sexually suggestive fashion. Actually, it was more explicit than suggestive. Melanie Singer wasn't so much fearful as offended.[11]

Juxtaposed against the videotape of the beating, Koon's description is ripe with racialized ululation. The conceptual set of the white woman, the "burly black male," and sexual innuendo is familiar territory. What contextualizes Koon's reading of this scene, then, is his inability to read King's actions based on his reaction to the black body. Witnessing his own myopia, Koon includes a "second-by-second" reading of the videotape prepared by another member of the Los Angeles Police Department. Opening nearly four minutes before the "use of force" begins, this narrative is silent about the sexualized performance Koon describes. King, then, becomes the racial and sexual minstrel in a performative text written and read by Koon.

I have said that white riot is accompanied by manipulations of power that pervert images of black people, thereby deriving images of black bodies that are hypersexualized and associated with violence. Nowhere are these images generated with as much tenacity as they are in Hollywood. What makes the legacy of Los Angeles so provocative is that it forces us to see cultural violence in different ways. When the diametrical opposition of black and white in American culture no longer defines it, the riot scene becomes morally complicated. Indeed, race long ago ceased to be an easily recognized dividing line. Consider, for instance, that although he does not dramatize how the multiethnic cultural mix complicates race difference in America, Charles Chesnutt spices *The Marrow of Tradition* with references to the Chinese and Jewish presence in Wilmington. As Ronald Takaki indicates, the race war in Los Angeles also had no racial borders.[12] To date there is only one fictionalized version of the Los Angeles Rebellion, Anna Deveare Smith's *Twilight: Los Angeles, 1992*. As Smith notes in her docudrama of the event, the "race riot" involved Americans of various racial and ethnic identities, including white Americans. In the aftermath of Los Angeles, where Hollywood images of American culture can no longer comfortably figure the race problem as an abiding conflict between black and white, there can remain no allusions about how we see ourselves.

MMABATHO: WHITE RIOT AND THE CALL TO ARMS

The white riot at Mmabatho may seem to be radically different from the other instances of riot violence that inform this study. However, this incident is the outgrowth of the same progression from racialized ululation to violence that erupted in Wilmington, Soweto, and Los Angeles. The violence drew an international audience, having been situated prominently in the news media. The account that best frames this as an incident of white riot is an article that was picked up by the Associated Press and disseminated worldwide. Entitled "Dictator Capitulates as Anarchy Grips South African Homeland," the article was written by Bob Drogin, the *Los Angeles*

Times reporter who witnessed the violence. The article was ostensibly about the capitulation of Lucas Mangope, then president of Bophuthatswana, who had refused to participate in the all-race elections and to support the reincorporating of the Bantustan into South Africa. However, Drogin devotes most of his attention to the three Afrikaner men who traveled to Mmabatho to fight to preserve the apartheid policy that was collapsing in South Africa. The images of the dead men dominate the description of the event and the photographs of the men almost comprise a photojournalistic account of it. Their bodies, dead and white, situate them as victims as does the tone of Drogin's account. After all, he reports their names and allows his audience to "converse" with the men just before their tragic deaths. The three men frame Drogin's vision of the racial violence; they are the protagonists of the story, victims of the violence. When he describes their deaths at the hands of a black police officer, he characterizes it as a "cold-blooded execution," committed by a "black man in a police uniform." Drogin shapes their narrative with the cover of gallantry while simultaneously placing black bodies at the center of the conflict.

Drogin's account is characterized by the ways in which the black body is imagined in violence and by the invisibility of white riot. Beginning with the ennobling portraits of Uys, Walfaardt, and Fourie, who came in response to the racialized ululation generated as the De Klerk government collapsed, Drogin uses his journalistic license to disassociate the men from the vicious violence he ascribes to the "roving bands of whites" later in the article. Throughout the article Drogin displaces white racialized violence from the bodies of the white men who inform the narrative, relishing the opportunity to describe the violence without naming them as perpetrators:

> At one point, several dozen youths ran down a street and through a field. Fast behind them was a pickup truck, with someone firing shots at the fleeing youths. By sunset, law and order had collapsed in the central business district.
> The only major skirmish occurred at about 12:45 p.m. at a dusty intersection just outside the city center.
> A convoy of 18 vehicles filled with right wingers roared by a road block set up by the Bophuthatswana army. Someone in the convoy fired into crowd of blacks, killing a woman. The soldiers ordered the group to stop; a tense stand-off ensued. Suddenly, fierce gunfire erupted. . . .
> All but the blue Mercedes escaped.[13]

Nothing is more telling than Drogin's tendency to associate the racialized violence with the numerous vehicles he describes in the article. It is as if the vehicles themselves—the car, the truck, the convoy, and the Mercedes—are riotous. Indeed, there is a something provocative about the Afrikaners'

Afrikaner resistance-movement supporters at the scene of Mmabatho's white riot, 11 March 1994 (AP/Wide World Photos)

choice to do battle in a Mercedes Benz. Not only is it a marker of their soon-to-be-lost economic and political power, it is a testimony to the power of whiteness at this point in South African history. There is a similar power dynamic implicit in Drogin's refusal to see them as rioters in their attempt to reassert white privilege in a literal black space, one created in the politics of apartheid as a place for black people. The power of not looking at the men as rioters is as significant as the ways in which Drogin attempts to look at them from a perspective influenced by his American heritage.

Drogin, however, is not the only witness to the deaths of these white rioters. NBC also covered the exchange, capturing the images of the masses of Afrikaner right wingers who came to defend white rights in Bophuthatswana. Interestingly, the news crew captures Uys, Walfaardt, and Fourie in the midst of their white riot. Standing behind the doors of their Mercedes, the news footage shows them shooting at the armed officers and the unarmed civilians at the scene. During the newscast of the events, true to the pattern I have already described, the network reported the event but turned its attention immediately to images of black bodies rioting and looting a local mall. The follow-up story aired on 13 March 1994, two days later. Elizabeth Vargas opened the 30-second news segment on the *NBC Evening News* referring to the fact that Bophuthatswana was under the direction of a white South African diplomat. What followed this opening underscores my insistence on the fact that rioting is always blackened at the discretion of the media. Vargas notes:

A white South African diplomat is in control of a black homeland tonight. Government troops patrolled the capitol of Bophuthatswana today when the deposed president tried to keep the homeland out of next month's first all-race elections. Meanwhile, outside of the homeland and inside of South Africa, there was black on black violence today when rival groups gathered at the same time for a political rally.

Both the *Los Angeles Times* story and the NBC broadcast suggest that white riot has been rendered so invisible that there is no language to portray it. The proximity of the white men to the violence is denied as strenuously as the black bodies are imprinted on the scene. The narrative of the violence begins and ends in images of the Afrikaner men, cloaked in a discourse that insists on white privilege and on the immediacy of black violence. Occurring as it did on the cusp of the literal and political millennium of South Africa, the systems that erased the realities of the white riot in Mmabatho may well color the possibilities of nonracialism in the new republic.

LEGACY OURS: A THING IN COMMON

Hall and Whannel indicate that with the repeated airing of violence, it comes to be "acknowledged as a 'natural' solution to difficult social problems." [14] American and South African cultures are certainly marked by episodes of racial violence that are the natural outgrowth of histories that cannot be separated from the legacy of apartheid. Both national borders are maintained by the tendency to racialize every colorized ethnicity while whiteness remains radically undefined except in terms of privilege. In America, the legacy of apartheid turns on white privilege and (mis)informs the rhetoric of cultural supremacy, a process that ultimately seeks to transform our notions of "racism," "sexism," and "political correctness" in order to endorse white privilege and to validate corroborating images, such as that of the white male as a beleaguered minority. When amnesty is the answer for race crimes committed in the passion of South African nationalism, race is the crime for which people of color are disproportionately sentenced. In South Africa, the legacy of apartheid is also clearly visible in the black-on-black violence, the outgrowth of the tribalist policies that enabled white supremacy (and which are also dangerously reminiscent of something familiarly American). The violence begs questions about the legacy of apartheid in the "new" South Africa. With a constitution that was once shaped with the American constitution in mind, can South Africa escape the racial quagmire that continues to trouble America?

Ultimately, race and culture collide in the legacy of apartheid, for the idea of race in these cultural contexts depends upon whatever racial pretensions are necessary to support white privilege. This work is my attempt to ensure that it will be possible to see beyond the racial perversions of the past and to recognize white riot for the mechanism of power that it is. When I first conceived of this project I had hoped to formulate a conclusion that would make white riot visible and attend to the association of violence with blackness, removing these constructs from the province of theoretical debate. In truth, though, there can be no conclusion to this project as long as the tie that binds American and South African cultures is racial violence.

Notes
Works Cited and Selected Bibliography
Filmography
Index

Notes

INTRODUCTION

1. Rodney King's none too eloquent plea of "Can we all just get along?" was made in the midst of the racial "unrest" that followed the acquittal of the Los Angeles Police Department officers who were accused of beating him on 3 March 1991. The fact that the question became a part of the rhetoric of the coverage of the unrest suggests that America's politics of racial division is conspicuous and abiding.

2. See Jacques Derrida, "But Beyond . . . (Open Letter to Anne McClintock and Rob Nixon)," in *"Race," Writing, and Difference,* ed. Henry Louis Gates, Jr. (Chicago: University of Chicago Press, 1986), 369.

3. Karla F. C. Holloway, *Codes of Conduct: Race, Ethics, and the Color of Our Character* (New Brunswick, N.J.: Rutgers University Press, 1995), 142.

4. I shall, both for the convenience of my argument and to approximate the racialized discourse which prefigures race riots, use *white* and *black* as racial categories in this study along with various other constructions of racial identity. *Whiteness* and *blackness* are necessarily contested terms, especially in the present cultural context in which Afrocentricity, Eurocentricity, and multiculturalism simultaneously essentialize and generalize these subject categories.

5. Homi K. Bhabha, "DissemiNation: Time, Narrative, and the Margins of the Modern Nation," in *Nation and Narration,* ed. Homi K. Bhabha (London: Routledge, 1990), 299.

6. Charles Chesnutt, *The Marrow of Tradition* (Ann Arbor: University of Michigan Press, 1969).

7. See Sipho Sepamla, *A Ride on the Whirlwind* (London: Heinemann, 1981). Because narratives of such events are too often reproduced out of context, these texts are silenced to the degree that they are mediated in analysis. As such, I see the inclusion of these texts as central to any understanding of the multiplicity of perspectives on racialized violence. See *Sarafina!,* dir. Darrell James Roodt, perf. Whoopi Goldberg, Miriam Makeba, Mbongeni Ngema, and Leleti Khumalo, Hollywood Studios, 1992; and *Cry Freedom,* dir. Richard Attenborough, perf. Kevin Cline, Penelope Wilton, and Denzel Washington, Universal Studios, 1987.

CHAPTER 1. RIOT-MAKING

1. Michael Parenti, *Power and the Powerless* (New York: St. Martin's Press, 1978), 85.

2. Noam Chomsky, *Necessary Illusions* (Boston: South End Press, 1989), 42.

3. Toni Morrison, *Playing in the Dark: Whiteness and Literary Imagination* (Cambridge: Harvard University Press, 1992), 16.

4. Maurice Evans, *Black and White in South East Africa* (New York: Negro Universities Press, 1969).

5. John Cell, *The Highest Stage of White Supremacy: The Origins of Segregation in South Africa and the American South* (New York: Cambridge University Press, 1982), 192.

6. George M. Fredrickson, *The Black Image in the White Mind* (New York: Harper and Row, 1971) and *White Supremacy: A Comparative Study in American and South African History* (New York: Oxford University Press, 1981), 250. Unfortunately, Fredrickson argues for another racialized fabrication: that the ancestors of both black and white South Africans migrated from sub-Saharan Africa and Holland at the same time. The notion that the most "native" South Africans are the Dutch is the crux of his argument.

7. Jacques Derrida, "But Beyond . . . (Open Letter to Anne McClintock and Rob Nixon)," in *"Race," Writing, and Difference,* ed. Henry Louis Gates, Jr. (Chicago: University of Chicago Press, 1986), 369.

8. Lewis Nkosi, "Minding South Africa," *Transition* 51 (1991): 240–45.

9. See Rob Nixon's *Homelands, Harlem and Hollywood: South African Culture and the World Beyond* (New York: Routledge, 1994).

10. When newly elected as president of South Africa, Nelson Mandela characterized South Africa as "new," although his administration had to address the social legacies of apartheid.

11. Although not an exhaustive listing, the following texts recognize the connection between these cultures: Keorapetse Kgositsile, "Notes from No Sanctuary" and "Point of Departure: Fire Dance Song," both in *Poems of Black Africa,* ed. Wole Soyinka (London: Heinemann, 1975), 89, and 204–7 respectively; André Brink, *Writing in a State of Siege* (New York: Summit Books, 1983); Mbulelo K. Mzamane, "Soweto Bride," in *Mzala: The Stories of Mbulelo Mzamane* (Johannesburg: Ravan Press, 1980), 125–45; Zakes Mofokeng, *A New Song: Totem Voices,* ed. Paul Carter Harrison (New York: Grove Press, 1989); Alex la Guma, *In the Fog of Season's End* (London: Heinemann, 1976); and Mazisi Kunene, "Thought on June 26" and "Tribute to Joan Baez on Vietnam," both in *Poems of Black Africa,* ed. Wole Soyinka (London: Heinemann, 1975), 208.

12. John Kisch and Edward Mapp, *A Separate Cinema* (New York: Farrar, Straus, and Giroux, 1992), 157. See also Peter Davis's *In Darkest Hollywood: Exploring the Jungles of Cinema's South Africa* (Athens: Ohio University Press, 1996), especially 38–47.

13. In 1947 the NAACP filed a petition detailing these grievances. W. E. B. DuBois was one of the architects of this document. Paul Robeson also appeared before the UN, charging the United States with genocide. Robeson's agitation for African American rights, especially his UN petition, made him the object of CIA

surveillance. This is one of the reasons that the Robeson family has maintained that his illness and subsequent death was the result of a government conspiracy.

14. V. Y. Mudimbe, *The Invention of Africa: Gnosis, Philosophy, and the Order of Knowledge* (Bloomington: Indiana University Press, 1988), 6.

15. In addition to Anthony Appiah, Henry Louis Gates, Jr., Cornel West, and Toni Morrison whom I consider at length here, a number of other African and African diaspora theorists have dealt with discourses on race. I do not consider this list to be all-inclusive, however, the following references are applicable: Adbul R. Jan-Mohamed in both "The Economy of Manichean Allegory: The Function of Racial Difference in Colonialist Literature," in *"Race," Writing and Difference*, ed. Henry Louis Gates, Jr. (Chicago: University of Chicago Press, 1986), 78–106 and *Manichean Aesthetics: The Politics of Literature in Colonial Africa* (Amherst: University of Massachusetts Press, 1983); Angela Davis, *Women, Race and Class* (New York: Random House, 1981); bell hooks, *Ain't I a Woman: Black Women and Feminism* (Boston: South End Press, 1982), and *Yearning: Race, Gender, and Cultural Politics* (Boston: South End Press, 1990); Hortense Spillers's introduction, "Who Cuts the Border? Some Readings on America" and Mae Henderson's "Toni Morrison's *Beloved*: Re-Membering the Body as Historical Text," both included in *Comparative American Identities: Race, Sex, and Nationality in the Modern Text*, ed. Hortense Spillers (New York: Routledge, 1991). Also, much of the cultural critiques of prominent scholars such as Houston Baker, Chinua Achebe, Ngugi Wa Thiong'o, and Frantz Fanon have also attended to the problematics of how the Western mind understands race and race difference.

16. Cornel West, *Prophesy Deliverance! An Afro-American Revolutionary Christianity* (Philadelphia: Westminister Press, 1982), 61.

17. This conflation of term and event is evident involving other marginalized groups. One example is the Five Points riot which occurred on 4 July 1857 in New York involving Irish immigrants. Although contemporary documents record their levels of dissatisfaction (according to a letter written by Anne Kennedy in 1858, New York "is a hell on erth [*sic*])," the Irish continue to immigrate in large numbers between 1845 and 1855. Their cultural makings: many did not speak English, they were Catholic, unskilled, and poor. In this situation, white (and there existed an ethnic difference between the Irish and other whites at this time) racialized violence also preceded the riot. The violence was precipitated by the disbandment of the New York City police department which ensured stricter enforcement of laws regulating the consumption of alcohol. A new unit, the Metropolitan Police, "which would answer only to the Assembly" replaced the local police. See Josh Brown and Bret Eynon, *Five Points: New York's Irish Working Class in the 1850's* (Ho-Ho-Kus, N.J.: American Social History Productions, 1987), 10.

18. What I suggest here is a term that describes a nomenclature consistent with the notion of violence perpetrated for a hegemonic cause, a "sterilized" notion of violence, such as that depicted in D. W. Griffith's ride of the KKK in *Birth of a Nation* (1915), or the ideologies participant in the concept of a white lie, hence, white violence.

19. Riot is also a figuration attributed to Morrison's "Africanist" presence, despite the fact that, as this analysis shows, the term is assigned to describe any episode of violence involving people of different races or ethnicities.

20. Although I limit the application of racialized ululation to specific histori-cal events in this text, this process can explain numerous movements of racialized violence. Examples include the representation of the Native American as barbaric, divided, and undeserving of their lands, which was not the initial reaction to or rep-resentation of the Native American. This ululation allows for numerous changes from the conquest of native lands and the establishment of reservations to the ne-cessity of being classified as "Indian" in order to receive federal protection. This is not unlike the mindset that accounts for the recent propensity to present the white male as a victim. Examples of this wave of ululation include the opening sequences of *Grand Canyon* (as Hazel Carby conceives of it) and Michael Douglas's film, *Fall-ing Down* (in terms of the right of white males to use violence to claim a space as "victims" in the midst of a colorized community of others), both of which defend white racialized violence in the same way as it is figured in the 1915 film *Birth of a Nation*.

21. Karla F. C. Holloway, *Codes of Conduct: Race, Ethics, and the Color of Our Character* (New Brunswick, N.J.: Rutgers University Press, 1995), 25.

22. Michael Eric Dyson, lecture, Vanderbilt University, 25 March 1999. See also Dyson's *I May Not Get There with You: The True Martin Luther King, Jr.* (New York: Free Press, 2000), especially 175–98.

23. If we consider the press as a form of political expression, it is interesting to note that the black press in Wilmington actually predated (by twelve years) the two majority presses that agitated for the violence in Wilmington in 1898.

24. Ann Allen Shockely, *Afro-American Women Writers 1746–1933* (New York: New American Library, 1988), 250. The editorial read, "Nobody in this section believes the old thread-bare lie that Negro men assault white women. If southern white men are not careful they will over-reach themselves and a conclusion will be reached which will be very damaging to the moral reputation of their women."

25. This is a thematic focus of African American literature, particularly in the twentieth century. See Gayl Jones, *Corregidora* (Boston: Beacon Press, 1975). Jones responds to this notion of revising history in the narration of the family history of her protagonist, Ursa Corregidora. Ursa, the last of the line of Corregidora women whose mother and grandmother were both fathered by the same Portuguese family patriarch, has a family history that is connected with the revisioning of white his-tory.

26. This is a connection that I wish to foreground although this is a subject that certainly needs to be problematized further. Prior to the abolition of slavery, the term *riot* was not used to describe interracial conflict. Instead, the terms *up-rising, revolt,* and *insurrection* are used to describe such violence. It is only after the Thirteenth Amendment when the social status of the majority of African Americans changed that race riot becomes the key term to reflect interracial conflict.

27. Serving Oakland, California.

28. Serving Kansas City, Missouri.

29. Serving New York, New York.

30. The name commonly associated with the San or Khosian people at this time was "Hottentot." They were the first to interact with the Dutch, thereby gaining the (perhaps dubious) distinction of liminality of being neither white nor black but "coloured." As early as 1658 with the introduction of slave labor in South Africa,

the Hottentots had acquired the legal designation of "coloured." This distinction continues not only with the social separation of the coloureds and blacks but as late as in the *South Africa 1993: Official Yearbook of the Republic of South Africa*, where they are listed separately from black South African ethnic groups.

31. Land ownership in this context did not relate to land as individually owned property. Rather, it was communal property to which nomadic groups had the right to freely migrate, hunt, and for those that herded, feed and graze stock. The debate about land ownership and the "vagrancy" of the coloureds is based on European definitions of land ownership and rights.

32. Ethnic identity as constructed by the government produced a dissonance in both the black and coloured communities. What is significant about the coloured experience is the trauma of not being "white." Two films in particular address this issue: *A Private Life* (1987) and *Mamza* (1985). See Martin Botha and Adri van Aswegen, *Images of South Africa: The Rise of the Alternative Film* (Pretoria: Human Sciences Research Council, 1992) for a detailed analysis.

33. The South African Institute of Race Relations has numerous references to the ambiguity arising from such racial definitions. See Ellen Hellmann and Henry Lever, eds., *Race Relations in South Africa, 1929–1979* (New York: St. Martin's Press, 1979).

34. Muriel Horrell, *Legislation and Race Relations* (Johannesburg: South African Institute of Race Relations, 1971), 111.

35. Individual suppression, prior to the repeal of the Apartheid Codes, included banning, which prohibited the individual from being in the company of more than two people (unless they are members of the immediate family), from writing documents for personal use or for publication, and allowed the government to remand the banned person to a specific province for residence.

36. Horrell, 111.

37. White ownership of the black press in the United States was also a factor. In fact, in the early 1900s, what came to be the dominant black journal in the United States, *Voice of the Negro*, was also white owned but staffed by blacks.

38. Hayden White, *Metahistory* (Baltimore: Johns Hopkins University Press, 1973), 31.

CHAPTER 2. READING THE RIOT ACT

1. Jack Thorne [David Bryant Fulton], *Hanover; or, The Persecution of the Lowly* (Wilmington: M. C. L. Hill, 1902).

2. Although neither the state trial on the original charges nor the federal trial on civil rights violation charges focused on the atmosphere of white supremacy as the reason for the assault, the issue was at the center of the controversy. Numerous articles written on the civil unrest center on this issue; however, the discourse of the rioters themselves provides the initial link.

3. Most black presses were weekly endeavors, especially due to the fact that newspapers depend upon advertising revenue to succeed. Wilmington had a black middle-class population sufficient to sustain the press through advertising revenues.

4. Felton later became the first woman elected to the U.S. Senate. See H. Leon Prather, Sr., *We Have Taken a City: Wilmington Racial Massacre and Coup of 1898*

(Rutherford, N.J.: Fairleigh Dickinson University Press, 1984), 70–72, and Eric Sundquist, *To Wake the Nations* (Cambridge: Belknap Press of Harvard University Press, 1993), 411–13. Felton's remarks were reprinted in broadsides and newspapers along the eastern seaboard from Georgia to New York. In fact, Manly was responding to a letter written about the speech to the editor of the *New York Times,* 17 August 1898.

5. Quoted in Prather, 71.

6. For an account of what was accepted interracial sexual politics, see "Blood Will Tell" in Neil R. McMillen's *Dark Journey* (Chicago: University of Illinois Press, 1990) and "Of Our Spiritual Strivings" in W. E. B. DuBois's *The Souls of Black Folk* (New York: Vintage Books, 1990).

7. There are no known extant copies of the 18 August 1898 *Record.* Ironically, were it not for the fact that the editorial was so often reprinted in white supremacist broadsides and in the white press, the editorial would be unavailable. See "White Women Slandered," Broadside, Elizabeth Moore Papers, New Hanover County Collection, North Carolina Department of Archives and History, Raleigh, N.C.

8. Ann Allen Shockley, *Afro-American Women Writers 1746–1933* (New York: New American Library, 1988), 245–61 and especially 248–61.

9. "Negro Rule in Craven County," Broadside, Elizabeth Moore Papers, New Hanover County Collection, North Carolina Department of Archives and History, Raleigh, N.C., 1898.

10. For a contemporary discussion of this issue, see bell hooks, *Yearning: Race, Gender, and Cultural Politics* (Boston: South End Press, 1990), 62–63.

11. Prather, 49–50.

12. Although the practice of displacing blame on the oppressed for their own oppression is not unique to this situation, the relationship of this practice to the riot event serves to define the cultural practice of race riots.

13. See Thomas W. Clawson, "The Wilmington Race Riot in 1898: Recollections and Memories." Louis T. Moore Papers, New Hanover County Collection, North Carolina Department of Archives and History, Raleigh, N.C.

14. Daniels was so influential that August Meier indicates that his "newspaper was . . . largely responsible for stirring up the Wilmington riot of 1898." See Meier, *Negro Thought in America 1880–1915* (Ann Arbor: University of Michigan Press, 1963), 81.

15. "Two More Fights at Pana," *New York Times,* 18 November 1898, 1.

16. This deceptive assessment of black male supernatural strength is repeated, almost verbatim, by white police officers in their assessment of Rodney King's injuries.

17. Andrew Howell, *The Book of Wilmington: 1730–1930* (1930; reprint, Wendell, N.C.: Broadfoots Bookmark, 1979), 183.

18. See Elizabeth F. McKoy, *Early Wilmington Block by Block from 1733 On* (Raleigh: Edwards and Broughton, 1967).

19. "Five Lessons for North Carolina Voters," Broadside, Elizabeth Moore Papers, New Hanover County Collection, North Carolina Department of Archives and History, Raleigh, N.C.

20. "Guns Still Coming to N.C.," *Wilmington Evening Dispatch,* 7 November 1898, 4.

21. Racial unity—black, white, and otherwise—is the focus of much speculation in any racialized culture. Black unity is shaped as unattainable in the United States, while hegemony characterizes the existence of white unity as unquestionable. Yet class issues threaten the dissolution of white alliance in interesting ways making the white poor—particularly welfare recipients, prostitutes, and the imprisoned—appear as anomalies rather than as a permanent part of the white underclass.

22. Prather, 87–89.

23. Evidence suggests that the *Record* was the only black daily newspaper in the nation at this time, although with the continual founding of black presses and the destruction of them by such supremacist movements, other black dailies may have been in existence. I use the term majority to refer to the white press.

24. Howell, 153.

25. According to census records, the wealth of the African American population exceeded that of whites in all except the upper economic class. Prather indicates that white unemployment was particularly high because employers preferred African American workers to white workers whom they perceived as wanting preferential treatment.

26. Josh Brown and Bret Eynon, *Five Points: New York's Irish Working Class in the 1850's* (Ho-Ho-Kus, N.J.: American Social History Productions, 1987), 10-11.

27. Ibid., 12.

28. For an extended discussion of Irish whiteness, see Noel Ignatiev, *How the Irish Became White* (New York: Routledge, 1995).

29. Meier, 20.

30. Manly had, in fact, long agitated for racial equality in Wilmington. In his determination to provide an alternative to the racialized ululation he and his contemporaries faced, he symbolized the precarious yet powerful agency of the black press. Due to his editorials unsanitary conditions in Brooklyn and Darktown—the African American sections in Wilmington—were corrected. He also exposed problems in the black ward of the county hospital. For a full discussion of this, see H. G. Jones, *North Carolina Illustrated, 1524-1984* (Chapel Hill: University of North Carolina Press, 1983) and Prather.

31. Prather, 69–70.

32. Hampton Institute was established along the educational model espoused by Booker T. Washington. In effect, students were trained in service-related fields.

33. The Sadgwar connection also provides an interesting cultural context. Sadgwar's paternal grandfather was David Elias Sadgwar, born the illegitimate son of a French sea captain and the daughter of a prominent white Wilmington family. Due to his illegitimate birth, Sadgwar was given to an enslaved African American woman to raise as her own. Consequently, he shared her slave status, despite the fact that he was white. He married Fanny Merrick, another enslaved woman with whom he attempted to flee to the North. Dressing his wife as a mammy, they left Wilmington with their two young children only to be returned as runaways and imprisoned. Because of the conditions at the prison (which was located across from the slave market on Fifth and Market Streets), both children died. After the war Sadgwar was given (it is not clear by whom) a plantation and eventually owned much of Fifth Street. One of his sons, Frederick Sadgwar, an architect and financier,

was the father of Carrie Sadgwar Manly. The Sadgwar family at one time owned the black newspaper in Wilmington. See also Prather and Jones.

34. Clawson, 8.

35. Interestingly, the *Record* office was relocated just across the street from the medical offices and pharmacy of Dr. Thomas R. Mask—whom Chesnutt fictionalizes as Dr. Will Miller—and his younger brother, John. Black businesses were most prevalent on Seventh Street south of Market Street. This move, despite the fact that he was forced from his lease by the machinations of Clawson and Waddell, probably exacerbated the problem for the leaders of the white riot because Manly relocated to an area that was just as economically supportive, if not more so, than his previous location.

36. In "The Case Stated," Ida B. Wells-Barnett elucidates the meaning of "inevitable" in this historical context. As Wells-Barnett notes, the political currency of "race riots" and "race rapes" shape the discourse about the urgency of white riot:

> During all the years of slavery, no such charge was ever made, not even during the dark days of the rebellion . . . . While the master was away fighting to forge the fetters upon the slave, he left his wife and children with no protectors save the Negroes themselves. . . . Likewise, during the period of alleged "insurrection," and alarming "race riot," it never occurred to the white man, that his wife and children were in danger of assault. Nor in the Reconstruction era, when the hue and cry was against "Negro domination," was there ever a thought that the domination would ever contaminate a fireside or strike to death the virtue of womanhood. It must appear strange indeed, to every thoughtful and candid man, that more than a quarter of a century elapsed before the Negro began to show signs of such infamous degeneration.

Quoted in Shockley, *Afro-American,* 258–59.

37. Rev. J. Allen Kirk, "A Statement of Facts Concerning the Bloody Riot in Wilmington, N.C.," [1900?], 3. The biblical text comes from Jeremiah 25:34–36: "Howl, ye shepherd, and cry; and wallow yourselves in the ashes, ye principal of the flock: for the days of your slaughter and of your dispersions are accomplished; and ye shall fall like a pleasant vessel. And the shepherds shall have no way to flee, nor the principal of the flock, shall be heard: for the Lord hath spoiled their pasture." Interestingly, what is left out are verses 37 and 38, two verses that might have quieted their commitment to incite unrest: "And the peaceable inhabitants are cut down because of the fierce anger of the Lord. He hath forsaken his covenant, as the lion: for their land is desolate because of the fierceness of the oppressor, and because of his fierce anger."

38. According to Prather, Manly family lore holds that Redshirt patrols in Wilmington gave Manly and his brothers weapons and told them to join the search for themselves.

39. Clawson, 8.

40. See *Wilmington: A Pictorial History,* Howell's *The Book of Wilmington,* and the extant copies of the *Wilmington Evening Dispatch* and *Wilmington Daily Messenger* for evidence of the "blame."

41. Clawson, 2–4.

42. Ibid., 8.

43. Clawson indicates that "Ten or twelve negroes lost their lives in the riot,

while two white men were seriously wounded" (4). Kirk relates numerous incidents of bodies but does not give an exact count, writing that "they went on firing . . . at every living Negro, killing a great many of them . . ." (10).

44. Kirk, 10.

45. There are graves in the cemetery that pre-date those from this era that are well maintained such as that of Prince LeBeau, an enslaved man who could "document" his regal ancestry. LeBeau escaped from being held by a cruel "master" and came to be "owned" by one of the governors of the North Carolina who had his "markings" analyzed. After the governor determined that LeBeau's "markings" were Arabic letters, he gave him an Arabic Bible.

46. Thorne, 95.

47. Editorial, *Wilmington Evening Dispatch*, 11 November 1898.

48. "Five Lessons for North Carolina Voters," Broadside.

49. Charles Chesnutt Papers, Fisk University Library Special Collections, Nashville, Tenn.

50. Ibid.

51. Klauss Ensslen, "Fictionalizing History: David Bradley's *The Chaneysville Incident*," *Callaloo* 11, no. 2 (1988): 281–96.

52. Helen Chesnutt, *Charles Waddell Chesnutt: Pioneer of the Color Line* (Chapel Hill: University of North Carolina Press, 1952), 1–10. Chesnutt, although arrested, was not prosecuted because the judge dismissed charges against him when he noted that his last name was misspelled as Chestnut on the arresting documents.

53. Chesnutt, *Marrow*, 51.

54. Ibid., 56–57.

55. Ibid., 60.

56. Ibid., 61.

57. Ensslen, 282.

58. M. M. Bakhtin, *The Dialogic Imagination*, ed. Michael Holquist, trans. Caryl Emerson (Austin: University of Texas Press, 1981), 370.

59. Quoted in Helen M. Chesnutt, *Charles Waddell Chesnutt*, 21.

60. The second work is *Paul Marchand, F.M.C.* [Free Man of Color]. Set in New Orleans of the 1820s, the novel—with its suggestion that "race" is a matter of cultural socialization rather than biology—was rejected for publication numerous times. It was published posthumously in 1998. See Charles Chesnutt, *Paul Marchand, F.M.C.* (Jackson: University Press of Mississippi, 1998). Chesnutt's *Wife of His Youth, and Other Stories of the Color Line* and *The House behind the Cedars* also detail the race relations in this era. *House* was, in fact, so popular that Oscar Micheaux, the foremost figure in early African American cinema, made two motion pictures based on this novel. In *The Wife of His Youth*, Chesnutt first uses the naming he employs in *Marrow* in the title character in "Uncle Wellington's Wives" and the use of a Front Street.

61. Here I borrow Chesnutt's phraseology to emphasize the intertextual relationship between Chesnutt and the community affected by the riot in Wilmington.

62. See Helen M. Chesnutt, *Charles Waddell Chesnutt*, 38. Market Street, named for the slave market that once stood at its center, marked the boundaries between blacks in Wilmington. The affluent north side and the working-class south side of the city were class-based spaces. Mask, of 409 North Seventh Street; Chesnutt, of

114 North Eighth Street; and Manly, residing in the Sadgwar residence at 15 North Eighth Street each had addresses that marked their prominence both in the city and in their race.

63. Charles Chesnutt to Mrs. W. E. Henderson, 11 November 1905, Chesnutt Papers.

64. J. E. Garford to Charles Chesnutt, 3 March 1901, Chesnutt Papers.

65. Charles Chesnutt to Thomas Hines Page, 11 November 1898, Chesnutt Papers. Though a white Southerner by birth, Page shared Chesnutt's concern about the "occurrences" in North Carolina in his response to Chesnutt dated 14 November 1898. He also confirms that the *Atlantic* did not release permission for Manly to reprint *The Wife of His Youth*.

66. Henry Louis Gates, Jr., *The Signifying Monkey* (New York: Oxford University Press, 1988), 69, 82, 124.

67. For an in-depth exploration of naming in African American literature, please see Kimberly W. Benston's "I Yam What I Am: The Topos of Un(naming) in Afro-American Literature," in *Black Literature and Literary Theory*, ed. Henry Louis Gates, Jr. (New York: Methuen, 1984), 165–66.

68. Chesnutt, *Marrow*, 141–42.

69. James Sprunt, *Information and Statistics Respecting Wilmington, North Carolina, Being a Report by the President of the Produce Exchange* (Wilmington: Jackson and Bell, Water-Power Presses, 1883), 238–39, 245–46.

70. Chesnutt, *Marrow*, 25.

71. Ibid.

72. "White Women Slandered," Broadside.

73. I thank Maurice Wallace for connecting Chesnutt's portrait of Delamere to the minstrel tradition.

74. Eric Lott, *Love and Theft* (New York: Oxford University Press, 1995), 118.

75. Chesnutt, *Marrow*, 270.

76. Sundquist, 441–42.

77. Chesnutt, *Marrow*, 47.

78. Prather, 89.

79. Chesnutt, *Marrow*, 303–4.

80. Robert Reinhold, "A Terrible Chain of Events Reveals Los Angeles without Its Makeup," *New York Times*, 3 May 1992, 4.1.

81. Karla K. C. Holloway, *Moorings and Metaphors: Figures of Culture and Gender in Black Women's Literature* (New Brunswick, N.J.: Rutgers University Press, 1992), 33.

82. Chesnutt, *Marrow*, 33–34.

83. McBane's historical counterpart is probably Hugh McRae, one of the Secret Seven. Chesnutt uses numerous references to McBane's "poor white" ancestry with illusions to his former occupation of overseer, like his father before him (81–82, 87). McBane's poor ancestry is traceable. The fact that there is not a land-owning McRae listed in the 1850 census, nor is there a mention of overseers by that name, is indicative of the poor ancestry to which Chesnutt refers. Chesnutt also insists that McBane is wealthy and lives in Wilmington as does McRae. Approximately eighteen overseers are listed in the 1850 census, with only one, John W. Biddle, listed as

being an immigrant. None, however, are listed as living in the city of Wilmington proper. See Eric Sundquist's *To Wake the Nations* for a fuller treatment of this.

84. Chesnutt, *Marrow*, 31.

85. Ibid., 33.

86. Prather, 87–88.

87. Sprunt, 79.

88. Chesnutt, *Marrow*, 243.

89. Ibid., 85.

90. Ibid., 89.

91. Prather, 212 and Meier, 162.

92. See James R. Grossman, *Land of Hope: Chicago, Black Southerners, and the Great Migration* (Chicago: University of Chicago Press, 1989), 32; and Walter C. Daniel, *Black Journals of the United States* (Westport, Conn.: Greenwood Press, 1982), 24.

93. Penelope Bullock, *The Afro-American Periodical Press, 1838–1909* (Baton Rouge: Louisiana State University Press, 1981), 66–67.

94. The masthead of the first issue read: "Edited by W. E. Burghardt DuBois, with the co-operation of Oswald Garrison Villard, J. Max Barber, Charles Edward Russell, Kelly Miller, W. S. Braithwaite and M. D. MacLean."

95. Eric Sundquist also comes to this conclusion in *To Wake the Nations*. My research situates Barber in the field prior to the publication of *Marrow* and uncovers the important links between Chesnutt and Barber.

96. Robert M. Farnsworth, introduction to Chesnutt, *Marrow*, x.

97. Chesnutt, *Marrow*, 294–95.

98. See Kelly Miller, "The Race Problem in the South," *Outlook* 60 (31 December 1898): 59–63.

99. DuBois writes: "In failing thus to state plainly and unequivocally the legitimate demands of their people . . . the thinking classes of American Negroes would shirk a heavy responsibility,—a responsibility to themselves, a responsibility to the struggling masses, a responsibility to the darker races of men whose future depends so largely on this American experiment." See DuBois, 45.

100. Chesnutt, *Marrow*, 8.

101. Chesnutt Papers.

102. *Morning Star*, 21 February 1911, 5.

103. DuBois, 39.

104. Chesnutt, *Marrow*, 181, 282, 295.

105. Ibid., 62.

106. Ibid., 299.

107. Ibid., 309.

108. Clawson, 3.

109. "Panic Stricken Negroes," *Wilmington Daily Messenger*, 11 November 1898, 1.

110. Misc. papers. Southern Historical Collections, University of North Carolina, Chapel Hill, N.C.

CHAPTER 3. RIOTING IN A STATE OF SIEGE

1. The author is currently in the process of compiling a volume of Chesnutt's essays, speeches, and observations about race.

2. Frank Welsh, *South Africa: A Narrative History* (New York: Kidansha International, 1999), 325.

3. Charles Chesnutt, "The Future American," *Boston Transcript,* 1 Sept. 1900, n.p., Charles Chesnutt Papers, Fisk University Library Special Collections.

4. Eric Lott, *Love and Theft* (New York: Oxford University Press, 1995), 132.

5. Ten such homelands were established in the 1970s. Each provided a "homeland" for the indigenous peoples based on language. They were: Bophuthatswana, established for the Tswana; Lebowa, established for the North Sotho; Gazankulu, established for the Shangaan and the Tsonga people; Venda, established for the Venda; KwaNgwame, established for the Swazi; QwaQwa established for the South Sotho; KwaZulu, established for the Zulu; Transkei and Ciskei, established for the Xhosa; and KwaNdebele, established for the South Ndebele.

6. As the 1994 all-race elections drew near, the "homelands" were reintegrated into South Africa. The first three homelands to be repatriated underwent the process as one of the results of preelection violence. Bophuthatswana, Ciskei, and KwaZulu were reintegrated into the republic after an Afrikaner invasion in Bophuthatswana resulted in numerous Afrikaner deaths.

7. Millard Arnold, ed., *Steve Biko: Black Consciousness in South Africa* (New York: Vintage Books, 1979), 107.

8. The problem of poor whites in South Africa is examined in sociological tracts most frequently before 1948 when the system of apartheid was established by Dr. H. F. Verwoerd. Macmillan's *Cape Colour Question* examines the issue, as does Maurice Evans in *Black and White in South East Africa* (New York: Negro Universities Press, 1969). Faced with class stratification in the white "community," Evans indicates that poor whites are a part of the black problem, that the very existence of the poor white is due to the existence of blacks in both South African and American society:

> It seems to me, that in the absence of this class in the country districts of the Northern States [of the United States], Canada, Australia, and New Zealand, and in its presence in the Southern States [of the United States] and South Africa, we must look for the reason in the one fundamental condition common to the two last and absent in the former; the presence of a servile race causing the white man to look upon labour, with its antiseptic medicinal virtues, as a degradation. (221)

See also Hermann Giliomee, "The Beginnings of Afrikaner Ethnic Consciousness, 1850-1915," in *The Creation of Tribalism in Southern Africa,* ed. Leroy Vail (Berkeley: University of California Press, 1989), 21-54. Giliomee indicates that, in addition to having British and Dutch ancestry, the Afrikaner also had German, French, and non-European (about 7 percent) ancestry.

I also do not want to suggest that the racial situation in South Africa is one in which blacks and whites are the only participants; however, these identities are the extremes around which all other social interaction is figured. As E. Feit indicates in "Community in a Quandary: The South African Jewish Community and Apartheid," *Race* 8 (1967): 403: "The best way of describing South African society is to say that it consists of groups of peoples brought together by history, all hating each other, but not enough to want to end their relationship."

9. Bhabha argues a similar point in "DissemiNation: Time, Narrative, and the Margins of the Modern Nation," in *Nation and Narration,* ed. Homi Bhabha (London: Routledge, 1990), 291–322. Specifically, Bhabha deals with the axis in terms of "the racist fantasy" (316) which is language based and dependent upon racist and sexist projection employed by the racist in the politics of defining identity.

10. See Muriel Horrell, *Legislation and Race Relations* (Johannesburg: South African Institute of Race Relations, 1971), 111. The Suppression of Communism Act, number 44 of 1950 was amended in 1962 and 1965.

11. Individual suppression, prior to the repeal of the Apartheid Codes, included banning, which prohibited the individual from being in the company of more than two people (unless they were members of the immediate family), from writing documents for personal use or for publication, and allowed the government to remand the banned person to a specific province as a place of residence.

12. In the Xhosa language the head of this section means, "What's bothering you, our child?"

13. M. Gatsha Buthelezi, "What Foreigners Must Know," in *Power Is Ours: Buthelezi Speaks on the Crisis in South Africa* (New York: Books in Focus, 1979), 129. Buthelezi, the former president of KwaZulu, was aligned with the white power structure of South Africa in intriguing ways. He established the Inkatha Freedom Party, ostensibly to salvage Zulu culture. Instead, Inkatha has been used by the government to foster tribalism. In the period leading up to the Soweto violence, Buthelezi was presented by the press as an opponent of the white government, the same white government that paid his salary as a homeland president. In the midst of the student uprising in Soweto, Zulu men were armed by the police and fought against the students and other demonstrators (see Magubane's *Soweto: The Fruit of Fear*).

In the political maneuvering surrounding the all-race elections in postapartheid South Africa, Buthelezi was presented as the alternative to Nelson Mandela. Interestingly enough, U.S. coverage of preelection black-on-black violence abruptly ceased after Buthelezi agreed to be a part of the elections.

14. Firinne Ni Chréacháin, "If I Were a Woman, I'd Never Marry an African," *African Affairs* 91 (1992): 245.

15. Angelina Mthenjane, personal interview, 15 June 1993.

16. Steve Biko [Frank Talk], "The Quest for a True Humanity," in *I Write What I Like,* ed. Aelred Stubbs (London: Heinemann, 1979), 91.

17. Jack Mthenjane, personal interview, 15 June 1993.

18. Robert Boyers et al., "A Conversation with Nadine Gordimer," *Salmagundi* 62 (winter 1984): 11.

19. Ibid.

20. The editorial statement of the *World* characterizes the racial composition of the papers as follows:

The *World* is the largest-selling newspaper in the non-White communications field south of the equator. Full of excitement and vigorous stories, the *World* has been telling South Africa's black African people all the news that's fit to print since 1932 . . . . White South Africans are a relatively small part in the editorial make-up of the newspaper and its sister publication, *Weekend World*. Only in the management field does White capital and expertise make its presence felt.

21. John D. Brewer, *After Soweto: An Unfinished Journey* (Oxford: Clarendon Press, 1986), 324.

22. Woods became politically aware under the tutelage of Steve Biko, who demonstrated that the South African liberal supported the range of apartheid practice, enjoyed the benefits of whiteness, and offered nothing to the non-whites with whom they ostensibly sympathized. See Woods's *Asking for Trouble: The Education of a White African* (Boston: Beacon Press, 1981).

23. John Imrie, "Pupil Trouble," *Rand Daily Mail*, 11 June 1976, 17.

24. Ibid.

25. "Riot—Kruger Speaks," *World*, 17 June 1976, A1.

26. Michael Parenti, *Power and the Powerless* (New York: St. Martin's Press, 1978), 150.

27. "Riots Rage—Army on Standby," *Rand Daily Mail*, 17 June 1976, A1.

28. Viv Prince, "Victim 'Loved Africans,'" *Rand Daily Mail*, 17 June 1976, A1.

29. The coverage in the *Mail* on 18 June 1976 is slanted to portray the "riotous" nature of the protesters. At the same time the targets outlined in each reference suggest that the students concentrated their efforts on those structures that represented the government. In "Firebug Mobs on Rampage beneath Soweto Smog," the actions of the students are described:

But by 7:30 am crowds began for the second day began [*sic*] gathering in the streets of Orlando and neighboring Diepkloof. Then the fires started for the second day in succession. Thick black smok [*sic*] rose from the blazing cars, while an almost misty brown billowed from the schools and public halls the rioters were destroying. (A5)

30. Vic Alhadeff, *A Newspaper History of South Africa* (Cape Town: Don Nelson, 1985), 131.

31. "Riot at Soweto," *Rand Daily Mail*, 17 June 1976, A1.

32. "Race War Possible," *World*, 3 June 1976, A3.

33. "Police Clash with Protest Marchers,'" *World*, 16 June 1976, extra late ed., A1.

34. The photograph of Peterson was taken by Sam Nzima who was then a photographer for the *World*. This photograph comes to represent the cruelty of the South African regime; it was literally reprinted around the world.

35. Photograph caption, *World*, 17 June 1976, A1.

36. Two other novels are concerned with the events in Soweto. Mbulelo Mzamane's *Children of Soweto* details the uprising through an autobiographical reconstruction of the events from the point of view of three narrators, one of whom is a white man caught in Soweto during the violence. The voice of the author is very much a part of the text. Miriam Tlali's *Amandla* concerns the lives of township resi-

dents a year after the uprising. According to Kelwyn Sole in "The Days of Power: Depictions of Politics and Community in Four Recent South African Novels" Tlali interweaves "several human interest stories" in the text to "present a number of area s of black discontent" (66). Sepamla's text is more useful to my discussion because he fictionalizes the events as they unfold in ways that enable the text to be a powerful protest novel.

37. In the midst of searching the home of a Sis Joyce, whose husband is involved in the uprising, Sepamla describes the exchange: " 'Look man, we are members of the police and you must tell us the "tru-truth." ' Sis Joyce knew all that, and the noise of the busy-bees in the other rooms confirmed it all. She elected to stare at the officers. Silence was her defense under the siege" (93–94). The scene exposes the whites perception that they control what is true in the culture. While they are looking for her husband, they question Joyce about the possibility that he has taken a lover. They pretend to read while not reading. In his rendering of their actions and their language contrasted against Sis Joyce's inaction and her silence, Sepamla explores their oppositional and culturally specific understanding of the truth.

38. Sepamla, 11.

39. Mbulelo V. Mzamane, "The Uses of Traditional Oral Forms in Black South African Literature," in *Literature and Society in South Africa,* ed. Landeg White and Tim Couzens (New York: Longman, 1984), 148.

40. Ibid., 147.

41. Sepamla, 33.

42. Ibid., 57.

43. Mashinini was the first president of the Student Representative Council.

44. Sepamla, 196.

45. Ibid., 60.

46. Ibid., 169.

47. Ibid.

48. Ibid., 22.

49. Ibid., 65.

50. Ibid., 21.

51. Ibid., 22.

52. Ibid., 242–43.

53. Mark Ralph-Bowman, "The Price of Being a Writer," *Index on Censorship* 11.4 (1982): 15–16.

54. "Censor's Report on *A Ride on the Whirlwind,*" *Index on Censorship* 12.3 (1983): 12.

55. Ibid.

56. Mzamane, "Traditional," 159.

57. Sepamla, 244.

58. Frank Molteno, "The Uprising of 16th June: A Review of the Literature on Events in South Africa 1976," *Social Dynamics* 5 (1979): 56.

CHAPTER 4. SUBVERTING THE SILENCES

1. Howard Kurtz, *Media Circus: The Trouble with America's Newspapers* (New York: Times Books, 1993), 76.

2. Chinua Achebe, "The Truth of Fiction," in *Hopes and Impediments* (New York: Anchor, 1988), 145.

3. See chapter 1.

4. Michael Chapman explores these issues peripherally in "Drum and Its Significance," in *The "Drum" Decade: Stories from the 1950's,* ed. Michael Chapman (Pietermaritzburg: University of Natal Press, 1989), 183–232.

5. Lewis Nkosi, "Encounter with New York 1," in *Home and Exile and Other Selections* (1965; reprint, New York: Longman, 1983), 58.

6. Anne McClintock, "'No Longer in a Future Heaven': Women and Nationalism in South Africa," *Transition* 51 (1991): 104–23.

7. J. M. Coetzee, *Age of Iron* (New York: Random House, 1990), 74.

8. Ibid., 194–95.

9. John Hope Franklin, *From Slavery to Freedom: A History of Negro Americans* (New York: Random House, 1969), 341.

10. Thomas W. Clawson, "The Wilmington Race Riot in 1898: Recollections and Memories," 5, Louis T. Moore Papers, New Hanover County Collection, North Carolina Department of Archives and History, Raleigh, N.C.

11. Mary Church Terrell, "From *A Colored Woman in a White World*," in *Bearing Witness: Selections from African-American Autobiography in the Twentieth Century,* ed. Henry Louis Gates, Jr. (New York: Pantheon Books, 1991), 58–59.

12. Ibid., 54.

13. Walter White, "*A Man Called White,*" in *Growing Up Black,* ed. Jay David (New York: Avon Books, 1968), 7–8.

14. Ibid., 9.

15. Ralph Ellison, *Invisible Man* (New York: Random House, 1952), 553.

16. Franklin, 474–75.

17. Toni Morrison, *Jazz* (New York: Alfred A. Knopf, 1992), 57.

18. Ibid.

19. Octavia Butler, *Kindred* (Boston: Beacon Press, 1979), 196.

20. For an analysis of the limitations of the industry as a medium of social change, see Martin Botha and Adri van Aswegen's *Images of South Africa: The Rise of the Alternative Film* (Pretoria: Human Sciences Research Council, 1992). South African film development is hampered, according to the *South Africa 1993: Official Yearbook of the Republic of South Africa,* by both dependence on "European and American products" and government and business manipulation of films.

21. Loren Kruger, "Staging South Africa," *Transition* 59 (1993): 120.

22. Botha and Aswegen, 71.

23. Dennis Beckett, foreword to Nomavenda Mathiane, *Beyond the Headlines: Truths of Soweto Life* (Johannesburg: Southern Book Publishers, 1990), vii.

24. As Donald Bogle indicates in *Toms, Coons, Mulattoes, Mammies, and Bucks* (New York: Continuum Publishing, 1990), Goldberg is the only black actress who is consistently cast in starring roles in the 1980s; however, her "films . . . usually treated her as an oddity, never placing her within a cultural context with which a black audience could identify" (297). Something about her is palatable to a white audience. Even before her embrace of black-face minstrelsy with Ted Danson, who was, at the time, her significant other, Goldberg was usually cast against a white male star, having little interaction with other blacks. Because of this, Goldberg is

recast in a minstrel tradition of her own which seemingly defines both her personal and private lives.

25. The ancestor relationship in indigenous religious practice is figured in Mazisi Kunene, "The Bond," in *Poems of Black Africa*, ed. Wole Soyinka (London: Heinemann, 1975), 47–48:

So many are asleep under the ground,
When we dance at the festival
Embracing the earth with our feet.

26. First was also one of the leaders in the antipass campaign who delivered a protest to the government offices against the laws. She was among a group of 20,000 women involved in the demonstration on 9 August 1956. The march is commemorated as "South Africa Women's Day." See the International Defence and Aid Fund for Southern Africa and UNESCO's *Fighting Apartheid: A Cartoon History* (London: IDAF Publications, 1987), 31.

27. Jack Mthenjane, personal interview, 15 June 1993. See also chapter 3.

28. Although Biko's death was not termed a suicide, the official cause of death was listed as a hunger strike. For an example of how the discourse of the racialized society rewrites the text of history, refer to "Inquest into the Death of Bantu Steve Biko," reprinted in Millard Arnold's *Steve Biko: Black Consciousness in South Africa* (New York: Vintage Books, 1979), 339–60.

29. *No Way Out*, dir. Joseph Mankiewicz, perf. Richard Wydmark, Linda Darnell, and Sidney Poitier, Twentieth Century-Fox, 1950.

30. Bogle, 222.

31. *Do the Right Thing*, dir. Spike Lee, perf. Spike Lee, Samuel L. Jackson, Ossie Davis, Ruby Dee, and Danny Aiello, Universal City Studios, 1989.

32. Ibid.

EPILOGUE

1. Michel Foucault, *Power/Knowledge: Selected Interviews and Other Writings, 1972–1977*, ed. Colin Gordon, trans. Colin Gordon et al. (New York: Pantheon Books, 1980), 123.

2. Howard Kurtz, *Media Circus: The Trouble with America's Newspapers* (New York: Times Books, 1993), 77.

3. Sheryl Brown, telephone interview by author, San Bernadino, Calif., 26 March 1993.

4. *Fear of a Black Hat*, dir. Rusty Cundieff, perf. Rusty Cundieff, Larry B. Scott, and Mark Christopher Lawrence. PolyGram Video, 1995.

5. Ice-T, *The Ice Opinion* (New York: St. Martin's Press, 1994), 47.

6. Steve Padilla and Leslie Berger, "Cameraman's Test Puts Him in the Spotlight," *Los Angeles Times*, 7 March 1991, B1.

7. According to the same article by Padilla and Berger, Josie Morales watched the beating as "the indicent unfolded." Morales also watched George Holliday as he prepared to videotape the scene. The article indicates that about twenty people watched the beating. Most of those interviewed were concerned for King's life.

Morales is also featured in Anna Deveare Smith's *Twilight: Los Angeles, 1992.* In fact, Padilla and Berger identify only three of the twenty witnesses they interviewed: Josie Morales, Dawn Davis, and Dorothy Gibson. Each of the women were able to interpret the situation unfolding before them. These women witnessed the event differently from Holliday who was "barely aware of what was unfolding."

8. Stuart Hall and Paddy Whannel, *The Popular Arts* (New York: Pantheon Books, 1965), 20.

9. Padilla and Berger, *Los Angeles Times,* 7 March 1991.

10. Stacey Koon, *Presumed Guilty: The Tragedy of the Rodney King Affair* (Washington, D.C.: Regnery Gateway, 1992), 41–42.

11. Ibid., 33.

12. Ronald Takaki, *Violence in the Black Imagination* (New York: Oxford University Press, 1993), 6.

13. Bob Drogin, "Dictator Capitulates as Anarchy Grips South African Homeland," *Los Angeles Times,* 12 March 1994, A15.

14. Hall and Whannel, 112.

Works Cited and
Selected Bibliography

Achebe, Chinua. *Hopes and Impediments*. New York: Anchor, 1988.

Alhadeff, Vic. *A Newspaper History of South Africa*. Cape Town: Don Nelson, 1985.

Anderson, James D. *The Education of Blacks in the South, 1860-1935*. Chapel Hill: University of Chapel Hill Press, 1988.

Appiah, Anthony. "The Conservation of Races." In *W. E. B. DuBois Speaks: Speeches and Addresses, 1890-1919*, ed. Philip Foner. New York: Path Press, 1977.

Appiah, Anthony. *Dusk of Dawn: An Essay toward an Autobiography of a Race Concept*. New York: Krause, 1975.

Appiah, Anthony. "The Uncompleted Argument." In *"Race," Writing, and Difference*, ed. Henry Louis Gates, Jr. Chicago: University of Chicago Press, 1986.

Arnold, Millard, ed. *Steve Biko: Black Consciousness in South Africa*. New York: Vintage Books, 1979.

Bakhtin, M. M. *The Dialogic Imagination*. Ed. Michael Holquist. Trans. Caryl Emerson and Michael Holquist. Austin: University of Texas Press, 1981.

Balbus, Isaac D. *The Dialectics of Legal Repression*. New York: Russell Sage Foundation, 1973.

Barksdale, Richard, and Keneth Kinnamon. *Black Writers of America*. New York: Macmillan, 1972.

Beckett, Dennis. Foreword to *Beyond the Headlines: Truths of Soweto Life*, by Nomavenda Mathiane. Johannesburg: Southern Book Publishers, 1990.

Berry, Mary Frances. *Black Resistance/White Law*. New York: Meredith Corporation, 1974.

Bhabha, Homi K. "DissemiNation: Time, Narrative, and the Margins of the Modern Nation." In *Nation and Narration*, ed. Homi K. Bhabha. London: Routledge, 1990.

Biko, Stephen. "Biko on Death." *New Republic* (7 January 1977): 12.

Biko, Stephen. [Frank Talk]. "The Quest for a True Humanity." In *I Write What I Like*, ed. Aelred Stubbs. London: Heinemann, 1979.

Bogle, Donald. *Toms, Coons, Mulattoes, Mammies, and Bucks*. New York: Continuum Publishing, 1990.

Botha, Martin, and Adri van Aswegen. *Images of South Africa: The Rise of the Alternative Film*. Pretoria: Human Sciences Research Council, 1992.

Bourdieu, Pierre. *In Other Words*. Trans. Matthew Adamson. Stanford: Stanford University Press, 1990.

Boyers, Robert, et al. "A Conversation with Nadine Gordimer." *Salmagundi* 62 (winter 1984): 3–31.

Brewer, John D. *After Soweto: An Unfinished Journey*. Oxford: Clarendon Press, 1986.

Brink, André. *Writing in a State of Siege*. New York: Summit Books, 1983.

Brittain, Victoria, and Abdul S. Minty. *Children of Resistance: Harare Conference on Children, Repression and the Law in Apartheid South Africa*. London: Kliptown Books, 1988.

Brooks, Alan, and Jeremy Brickhill. *Whirlwind before the Storm*. London: International Defence and Aid Fund for Southern Africa, 1980.

Brown, Josh, and Bret Eynon. *Five Points: New York's Irish Working Class in the 1850's*. Ho-Ho-Kus, N.J.: American Social History Productions, 1987.

Brown, Sheryl. Interview by author, 26 March 1993, San Bernadino, Calif. Transcript, *Black Voices News* office.

Bullock, Penelope. *The Afro-American Periodical Press, 1838–1909*. Baton Rouge: Louisiana State University Press, 1981.

Buthelezi, M. Gatsha. *Power Is Ours: Buthelezi Speaks on the Crisis in South Africa*. New York: Books in Focus, 1979.

Butler, Jeffrey. "Afrikaner Women and the Creation of Ethnicity." In *The Creation of Tribalism in Southern Africa*, ed. Leroy Vail. Berkeley: University of California Press, 1989.

Butler, Octavia. *Kindred*. Boston: Beacon Press, 1979.

Cell, John. *The Highest Stage of White Supremacy: The Origins of Segregation in South Africa and the American South*. New York: Cambridge University Press, 1982.

"Censor's Report on *A Ride on the Whirlwind*." *Index on Censorship* 12.3 (1983): 12.

Cesaire, Aime. *Lettre a Maurice Thorez*. Paris: Presence Africaine, 1956.

Chapman, Abraham. *Black Voices*. New York: New American Library, 1968.

Chapman, Michael. *The "Drum" Decade: Stories from the 1950's*. Pietermaritzburg: University of Natal Press, 1989.

Chesnutt, Charles. Charles Chesnutt Papers. Fisk University Library Special Collections. Nashville, Tenn.

Chesnutt, Charles. "The Future American." *Boston Transcript*. 1 September 1900. Charles Chesnutt Papers. Fisk University Library Special Collections. Nashville, Tenn.

Chesnutt, Charles. *The House behind the Cedars*. New York: Houghton Mifflin & Company, 1900.

Chesnutt, Charles. *The Marrow of Tradition*. Ann Arbor: University of Michigan Press, 1969.

Chesnutt, Charles. *Paul Marchand, F.M.C.* Jackson: University Press of Mississippi, 1998.

Chesnutt, Charles. *The Wife of His Youth, and Other Stories of the Color Line*. Ann Arbor: University of Michigan Press, 1968.

Chesnutt, Helen. *Charles Waddell Chesnutt: Pioneer of the Color Line.* Chapel Hill: University of North Carolina Press, 1952.

Chikota, Richard A. *Riot in the Cities: An Analytical Symposium of Causes and Effects.* Rutherford, N.J.: Fairleigh Dickinson University Press, 1970.

Chomsky, Noam. *Necessary Illusions.* Boston: South End Press, 1989.

Chréacháin, Firinne Ni. "If I Were a Woman, I'd Never Marry an African." *African Affairs* 91 (1992): 241–47.

Clawson, Thomas. "The Wilmington Race Riot in 1898: Recollections and Memories." Louis T. Moore Papers. New Hanover County Collection, North Carolina Department of Archives and History, Raleigh, N.C.

Cobbing, Julian. "The Mfecane as Alibi: Thoughts on Dithakong and Mbolompo." *Journal of African History* 29 (1988): 487–519.

Coetzee, J. M. *Age of Iron.* New York: Random House, 1990.

Couzens, Tim. "The Ghostly Dance of Bloodless Categories: Research in South African Literature." In *The Ghostly Dance: Writing in a New South Africa.* Mowbray: Institute for a Democratic Alternative for South Africa, 1990.

Crenshaw, Kimberle, and Gary Peller. "Reel Time / Real Justice." In *Reading Rodney King: Reading Urban Uprising.* New York: Routledge, 1993.

Daniel, Walter C. *Black Journals of the United States.* Westport, Conn.: Greenwood Press, 1982.

Davidson, Basil. *The Black Man's Burden: Africa and the Curse of the Nation-State.* New York: Times Books, 1992.

Davis, Angela. *Women, Race and Class.* New York: Random House, 1981.

Davis, Ossie. Preface to *We Charge Genocide,* ed. William L. Patterson. New York: International Publishers, 1951.

Davis, Peter. *In Darkest Hollywood: Exploring the Jungles of Cinema's South Africa.* Athens: Ohio University Press, 1996.

Derrida, Jacques. "But Beyond . . . (Open Letter to Anne McClintock and Rob Nixon)." In *"Race," Writing, and Difference,* ed. Henry Louis Gates, Jr. Chicago: University of Chicago Press, 1986.

DuBois, W. E. B. *The Souls of Black Folk.* New York: Vintage Books, 1990.

Duke, Michael, ed. *The Negro Almanac: A Reference Work on the Afro-American.* Bicentennial edition. New York: Bellwether Publishing, 1976.

Dyson, Michael Eric. *I May Not Get There with You: The True Martin Luther King, Jr.* New York: Free Press, 2000.

Dyson, Michael Eric. Lecture. Vanderbilt University. 25 March 1999.

Eaton, Hubert A. *Every Man Should Try.* Wilmington: Bonaparte Press, 1984.

Ebony Pictorial History of Black America. Vols. 1–3. Nashville: Southwestern Company, 1971.

Elizabeth Moore Papers. New Hanover County Collection, North Carolina Department of Archives and History, Raleigh, N.C.

Ellison, Ralph. *Invisible Man.* New York: Random House, 1952.

Ensslen, Klaus. "Fictionalizing History: David Bradley's *The Chaneysville Incident.*" *Callalloo* 11, no. 2 (1988): 281–96.

Evans, Maurice. *Black and White in South East Africa.* New York: Negro Universities Press, 1969.

Fair, Jo Ellen, and Roberta J. Astroff. "Constructing Race and Violence: U.S. News

Coverage and the Signifying Practices of Apartheid." *Journal of Communications* 41.4 (1991): 58–74.

Fanon, Frantz. *The Wretched of the Earth.* New York: Grove Weidenfeld, 1968.

Farnsworth, Robert M. Introduction to *The Marrow of Tradition.* Ann Arbor: University of Michigan Press, 1969.

Feit, E. "Community in a Quandary: The South African Jewish Community and Apartheid." *Race* 8 (1967): 401–15.

"Firebug Mobs on Rampage beneath Soweto Smog." *Rand Daily Mail,* 18 June 1976, A5.

"Five Lessons for North Carolina Voters." Broadside (circulated in 1898). Elizabeth Moore Papers. New Hanover County Collection, North Carolina Department of Archives and History, Raleigh, N.C.

Foucault, Michel. *The Archeology of Knowledge.* New York: Pantheon Books, 1982.

Foucault, Michel. *The Order of Things.* New York: Pantheon Books, 1973.

Foucault, Michel. *Power/Knowledge: Selected Interviews and Other Writings, 1972– 1977.* Ed. Colin Gordon. Trans. Colin Gordon, Leo Marshall, John Mepham, and Kate Soper. New York: Pantheon Books, 1980.

Franklin, John Hope. *From Slavery to Freedom: A History of Negro Americans.* New York: Vintage Books, 1969.

Fredrickson, George M. *The Black Image in the White Mind.* New York: Harper and Row, 1971.

Fredrickson, George M. *White Supremacy: A Comparative Study in American and South African History.* New York: Oxford University Press, 1981.

Gates, Henry Louis, Jr., ed. *"Race," Writing, and Difference.* Chicago: University of Chicago Press, 1986.

Gates, Henry Louis, Jr., ed. *The Signifying Monkey.* New York: Oxford University Press, 1988.

Giliomee, Hermann. "The Beginnings of Afrikaner Ethnic Consciousness, 1850– 1915." In *The Creation of Tribalism in Southern Africa,* ed. Leroy Vail. Berkeley: University of California Press, 1989.

Gooding-Williams, Robert. *Reading Rodney King: Reading Urban Uprising.* New York: Routledge, 1993.

Graves, Mae Blake. *1850 Federal Census of New Hanover County North Carolina.* Wilmington: n.p., 1982.

Grossman, James R. *Land of Hope: Chicago, Black Southerners, and the Great Migration.* Chicago: University of Chicago Press, 1989.

Gwaltney, John Langston. *Drylongso.* New York: Vintage Books, 1980.

Hall, Stuart, and Paddy Whannel. *The Popular Arts.* New York: Pantheon Books, 1965.

Harper, Michael. "The Book of Names." In *Black Literature and Literary Theory,* ed. Henry Louis Gates, Jr. New York: Methuen, 1984.

Hawk, Beverly, ed. *Africa's Media Image.* Westport: Praeger, 1992.

Heermance, J. Noel. *Charles W. Chesnutt: America's First Great Black Novelist.* Hamden, Conn.: Archon Books, 1974.

Hegel, Georg. *The Philosophy of History.* New York: Dover, 1956.

Heidegger, Martin. *Being and Time.* Trans. John Macquarrie and Edward Robinson. San Francisco: Harper and Row, 1962.

Hellmann, Ellen, and Henry Lever, eds. *Race Relations in South Africa 1929-1979.* New York: St. Martin's Press, 1979.

Henderson, Mae. "Toni Morrison's *Beloved:* Re-Membering the Body as Historical Text." In *Comparative American Identities: Race, Sex, and Nationality in the Modern Text,* ed. Hortense Spillers. New York: Routledge, 1991.

Hofmeyr, Isabel. "The Status of Oral Literature." In *The Ghostly Dance: Writing in a New South Africa.* Mowbray: Institute for a Democratic Alternative for South Africa, 1990.

Holloway, Karla F. C. *Codes of Conduct: Race, Ethics, and the Color of Our Character.* New Brunswick, N.J.: Rutgers University Press, 1995.

Holloway, Karla F. C. *Moorings and Metaphors: Figures of Culture and Gender in Black Women's Literature.* New Brunswick, N.J.: Rutgers University Press, 1992.

hooks, bell. *Ain't I a Woman: Black Women and Feminism.* Boston: South End Press, 1982.

hooks, bell. *Yearning: Race, Gender, and Cultural Politics.* Boston: South End Press, 1990.

Horrell, Muriel. *Legislation and Race Relations.* Johannesburg: South African Institute of Race Relations, 1971.

Howell, Andrew J. *The Book of Wilmington: 1730-1930.* 1930. Reprint, Wendell, N.C.: Broadfoots Bookmark, 1979.

Ice-T. *The Ice Opinion.* New York: St. Martin's Press, 1994.

Ignatiev, Noel. *How the Irish Became White.* New York: Routledge, 1995.

International Defence and Aid Fund for Southern Africa and UNESCO. *Fighting Apartheid: A Cartoon History.* London: IDAF Publications, 1987.

Isaacs, I. J., compiler. *Wilmington Up-To-Date.* Wilmington, N.C.: W. L. DeRosset, Jr., 1902.

JanMohamed, Abdul. "The Economy of Manichean Allegory: The Function of Racial Difference in Colonialist Literature." In *"Race," Writing, and Difference,* ed. Henry Louis Gates, Jr. Chicago: University of Chicago Press, 1986.

JanMohamed, Abdul. *Manichean Aesthetics: The Politics of Literature in Colonial Africa.* Amherst: University of Massachusetts Press, 1983.

Jeffery, Anthea. *Riot Policing in Perspective.* Johannesburg: South African Institute of Race Relations, 1991.

Jones, Gayl. *Corregidora.* Boston: Beacon Press, 1975.

Jones, H. G. *North Carolina Illustrated, 1524-1984.* Chapel Hill: University of North Carolina Press, 1983.

Jordan, Winthrop D. *Tumult and Silence at Second Creek.* Baton Rouge: Louisiana State University Press, 1993.

Judy, R. A. T. "Kant and the Negro." *Sapina Newsletter* 3.1 (January–July 1991): 1–57.

Kant, Immanuel. *Observations on the Feeling of the Beautiful and Sublime.* Trans. John T. Goldwait. Berkeley: University of California Press, 1960.

Keller, Frances Richardson. *An American Crusade: The Life of Charles Waddell Chesnutt.* Provo: Brigham Young University Press, 1978.

Kgositsile, Keorapetse. "Notes from No Sanctuary." In *Poems of Black Africa,* ed. Wole Soyinka. London: Heinemann, 1975.

Kgositsile, Keorapetse. "Point of Departure: Fire Dance Song." In *Poems of Black Africa,* ed. Wole Soyinka. London: Heinemann, 1975.

Kirk, Rev. J. Allen. "A Statement of Facts Concerning the Bloody Riot in Wilmington, N.C." [1900?].

Kisch, John, and Edward Mapp. *A Separate Cinema.* New York: Farrar, Straus, and Giroux, 1992.

Koon, Stacey. *Presumed Guilty: The Tragedy of the Rodney King Affair.* Washington, D.C.: Regnery Gateway, 1992.

Kouser, J. Morgan. *The Shaping of Southern Politics.* New Haven, Conn.: Yale University Press, 1974.

Kovel, Joel. *White Racism: A Psychohistory.* New York: Pantheon Books, 1970.

Kruger, Loren. "Staging South Africa." *Transition* 59 (1993): 120–29.

Kunene, Mazisi. "The Bond." In *Poems of Black Africa,* ed. Wole Soyinka. London: Heinemann, 1975.

Kunene, Mazisi. "Thought on June 26." In *Poems of Black Africa,* ed. Wole Soyinka. London: Heinemann, 1975.

Kunene, Mazisi. "Tribute to Joan Baez." In *Poems of Black Africa,* ed. Wole Soyinka. London: Heinemann, 1975.

Kurtz, Howard. *Media Circus: The Trouble with America's Newspapers.* New York: Times Books, 1993.

la Guma, Alex. *In the Fog of Season's End.* London: Heinemann, 1976.

Lodge, Tom. *Black Politics in South Africa since 1945.* New York: Longman, 1983.

Lott, Eric. *Love and Theft.* New York: Oxford University Press, 1995.

Lukacs, George. *The Theory of the Novel.* Trans. Anna Bostock. Cambridge: Massachusetts Institute of Technology Press, 1986.

Macmillan, W. M. *The Cape Colour Question.* London: Faber and Gwyer, 1927.

Magubane, Peter. *Soweto: The Fruit of Fear.* Trenton, N.J.: Africa World Press, 1986.

Manly, A. L. *Wilmington Daily Record,* 26 March 1898:1.

Manzo, Kate. "The Limits of Liberalism." *Transition* 55 (1992): 115–24.

Mathiane, Nomavenda. *Beyond the Headlines: Truths of Soweto Life.* Johannesburg: Southern Book Publishers, 1990.

McClintock, Anne. "'No Longer in a Future Heaven': Women and Nationalism in South Africa." *Transition* 51 (1991): 104–23.

McKoy, Elizabeth F. *Early Wilmington Block by Block from 1733 On.* Raleigh, N.C.: Edwards and Broughton, 1967.

McMillen, Neil R. *Dark Journey.* Chicago: University of Illinois Press, 1990.

Meier, August. *Negro Thought in America 1880–1915.* Ann Arbor: University of Michigan Press, 1963.

Melville, Herman. "Benito Cereno." In *The American Tradition in Literature,* ed. George Perkins et al. New York: Random House, 1985.

Metts, O. Van B. Letter. 1900. North Carolina Collection, University of North Carolina, Chapel Hill.

Miller, Kelly. "The Race Problem in the South." *Outlook* 60 (31 December 1898): 59–63.

Mkhondo, Rich. *Reporting South Africa.* London: James Currey, 1993.

Mofokeng, Zakes. *A New Song: Totem Voices.* Ed. Paul Carter Harrison. New York: Grove Press, 1989.

Molteno, Frank. "The Uprising of 16th June: A Review of the Literature on Events in South Africa 1976." *Social Dynamics* 5 (1979): 56–57.

Morris, Charles. "The Wilmington Massacre." In *The Voice of Black America: Major Speeches by Negroes in the United States, 1797–1971,* ed. Philip S. Foner. New York: Simon and Schuster, 1972.

Morrison, Toni. *Jazz.* New York: Alfred A. Knopf, 1992.

Morrison, Toni. *Playing in the Dark: Whiteness and the Literary Imagination.* Cambridge: Harvard University Press, 1992.

Mthenjane, Angelina. Interview with the author. 15 June 1993.

Mthenjane, Jack. Interview with the author. 15 June 1993.

Mudimbe, V. Y. *The Invention of Africa: Gnosis, Philosophy, and the Order of Knowledge.* Bloomington: Indiana University Press, 1988.

Mzamane, Mbulelo V. *Children of Soweto.* Johannesburg: Ravan Press, 1982.

Mzamane, Mbulelo V. *Mzala: The Stories of Mbulelo Mzamane.* Johannesburg: Ravan Press, 1980.

Mzamane, Mbulelo V. "The Uses of Traditional Oral Forms in Black South African Literature." In *Literature and Society in South Africa,* ed. Landeg White and Tim Couzens. New York: Longman, 1984.

Ndebele, Njabulo. "How Representative Is South African Literature?" In *The Ghostly Dance: Writing in a New South Africa.* Mowbray: Institute for a Democratic Alternative for South Africa, 1990.

Neal, Larry. "New Space / the Growth of the Black Consciousness in the Sixties." In *The Black Seventies,* ed. Floyd B. Barbour. Boston: Porter Sargent, 1970.

"Negro Rule in Craven County." Broadside (circulated in 1898). Elizabeth Moore Papers, New Hanover County Collection, North Carolina Department of Archives and History. Raleigh, N.C.

Nixon, Rob. *Homelands, Harlem and Hollywood: South African Culture and the World Beyond.* New York: Routledge, 1994.

Nkosi, Lewis. "Encounter with New York 1." In *Home and Exile and Other Selections.* 1965. Reprint, New York: Longman, 1983.

Nkosi, Lewis. "Minding South Africa." *Transition* 51 (1991): 240–45.

Outlaw, Lucius. "On W. E. B. DuBois' 'Conservation of Races.'" *Sapina Newsletter* 4.1 (January–July 1992): 13–28.

Parenti, Michael. *Power and the Powerless.* New York: St. Martin's Press, 1978.

Parry, Benita. "Culture Clash." *Transition* 55 (1992): 125–34.

Plato. *Republic.* Trans. G. M. A. Grube. Indianapolis: Hackett Publishing, 1974.

Prather, H. Leon, Sr. *We Have Taken a City: Wilmington Racial Massacre and Coup of 1898.* Rutherford, N.J.: Fairleigh Dickinson University Press, 1984.

The President's Initiative on Race Advisory Board. *One America in the 21st Century: Forging a New Future.* Washington, D.C.: Government Printing Office, 1998.

Ralph-Bowman, Mark. "The Price of Being a Writer." *Index on Censorship* 11.4 (1982): 15–16.

Reinhold, Robert. "A Terrible Chain of Events Reveals Los Angeles without Its Makeup." *New York Times,* 3 May 1992, sec. 4: 1+.

Render, Sylvia Lyons. *Charles Waddell Chesnutt*. Boston: Twayne Publishers, 1980.

Report of the Independent Commission on the Los Angeles Police Department, by Warren Christopher, chairman. Los Angeles: Independent Commission on the Los Angeles Police Department, 1991.

Riley, Eileen. *Major Political Events in South Africa 1948–1990*. Oxford: Facts on File, 1991.

Rule, James B. *Theories of Civil Violence*. Berkeley: University of California Press, 1988.

Sepamla, Sipho. *A Ride on the Whirlwind*. London: Heinemann, 1981.

Shockely, Ann Allen. *Afro-American Women Writers 1746–1933*. New York: New American Library, 1988.

Small, Adam. "In the Crucible: A Situation of Change for South African Literature." In *Race Relations in South Africa 1929–1979*, ed. Ellen Hellmann and Henry Lever. New York: St. Martin's Press, 1979.

Smith, Anna Deveare. *Twilight: Los Angeles, 1992*. New York: Anchor Books, 1994.

Sole, Kelwyn. "The Days of Power: Depictions of Politics and Community in Four Recent South African Novels." *Research in African Literatures* 19.1 (1988): 65–88.

Sole, Kelwyn. "Writing: Questions of Organisation and Democracy." In *The Ghostly Dance: Writing in a New South Africa*. Mowbray: Institute for a Democratic Alternative for South Africa, 1990.

South Africa 1993: Official Yearbook of the Republic of South Africa. Ed. Elise Keyter. Pretoria: South African Communication Service, 1993.

Sparks, Allister. *The Mind of South Africa*. New York: Alfred Knopf, 1990.

Sprunt, James. *Information and Statistics Respecting Wilmington, North Carolina, Being a Report by the President of the Produce Exchange*. Wilmington: Jackson and Bell, Water-Power Presses, 1883.

Suggs, Henry Lewis. *The Black Press in the South, 1865–1979*. Westport, Conn.: Greenwood Press, 1983.

Sundquist, Eric. *To Wake the Nations*. Cambridge: Belknap Press of Harvard University Press, 1993.

Switzer, Les. *Power and Resistance in an African Society*. Madison: University of Wisconsin Press, 1993.

Takaki, Ronald. *Violence in the Black Imagination*. New York: Oxford University Press, 1993.

Terrell, Mary Church. "From *A Colored Woman in a White World*." In *Bearing Witness: Selections from African-American Autobiography in the Twentieth Century*, ed. Henry Louis Gates, Jr. New York: Pantheon Books, 1991.

Thompson, Julius E. *The Black Press in Mississippi, 1865–1985*. Gainesville: University Press of Florida, 1993.

Thorne, Jack [David Bryant Fulton]. *Hanover; or, The Persecution of the Lowly*. Wilmington, N.C.: M. C. L. Hill, 1902.

Tlali, Miriam. *Amandla*. Johannesburg: Ravan, 1980.

Truth and Reconciliation Commission of South Africa. *The Truth and Reconciliation Commission of South Africa Report*. October 1998.

Vail, Leroy, ed. *The Creation of Tribalism in Southern Africa*. Berkeley: University of California Press, 1989.

Welsh, Frank. *South Africa: A Narrative History.* New York: Kidansha International, 1999.

West, Cornel. *Prophesy Deliverance! An Afro-American Revolutionary Christianity.* Philadelphia: Westminister Press, 1982.

West, Cornel. *Race Matters.* Boston: Beacon Press, 1993.

White, Hayden. *Metahistory.* Baltimore: Johns Hopkins University Press, 1973.

White, Walter. "*A Man Called White.*" In *Growing Up Black,* ed. Jay David. New York: Avon Books, 1968.

"White Women Slandered." Broadside (circulated in 1898). Elizabeth Moore Papers, New Hanover County Collection, North Carolina Department of Archives and History. Raleigh, N.C.

Woods, Donald. *Asking for Trouble: The Education of a White African.* Boston: Beacon, 1981.

Filmography

Bopha! Dir. Morgan Freeman. Perf. Danny Glover, Alfre Woodard, Malcolm Mc-
Dowell, and Marius Weyers. Miramax, 1993.
Cry Freedom. Dir. Richard Attenborough. Perf. Kevin Kline, Denzel Washington,
and Penelope Wilton. Universal Studios, 1987.
Cry, the Beloved Country. Dir. Zoltan Korda. Perf. Canada Lee, Sidney Poitier, and
Charles Carson. Lopert Films, 1952.
Cry, the Beloved Country. Dir. Darrell James Roodt. Perf. Richard Harris, James
Earl Jones, and Charles Dutton. Miramax, 1995.
Do the Right Thing. Dir. Spike Lee. Perf. Spike Lee, Samuel L. Jackson, Danny
Aiello, Ossie Davis, and Ruby Dee. Universal City Studios, 1989.
Fear of a Black Hat. Dir. Rusty Cundieff. Perf. Rusty Cundieff, Larry B. Scott, and
Mark Christopher Lawrence. PolyGram Video, 1995.
No Way Out. Dir. Joseph Mankiewicz. Perf. Richard Wydmark, Linda Darnell, and
Sidney Poitier. Twentieth Century-Fox, 1950.
Riot. Dir. Buzz Kulik. Perf. Jim Brown, Gene Hackman, Ben Carruthers, and Mike
Kellin. Universal Studios, 1969.
Rosewood. Dir. John Singleton. Perf. Ving Rhames, Jon Voight, Don Cheadle, and
Esther Rolle. Warner Bros., 1997.
Sarafina! Dir. Darrell James Roodt. Perf. Whoopi Goldberg, Leleti Khumalo,
Miriam Makeba, and Mbongeni Ngema. Hollywood Studios, 1992.

Index

Achebe, Chinua, 94, 105
African American literature, 26, 27, 28, 51–52, 54–55, 100–101, 102. *See also specific author or writing*
African Americans: as editors, 64–65; as filmmakers, 110–15; as poets, 26; as writers, 97–98, 101–5. *See also specific person*
Afrikaans, 29, 76, 78, 82
Afrikaners, 8, 28–29, 72, 88, 96–97, 106, 124–26
Age of Iron (Coetzee), 96–97, 105
Alhadeff, Vic, 82
ancestors, 108
apartheid: blackness as threat in, 90; and blacks as types, 114; black women in, 89; and censorship, 95; codification of, 29; connection between South African and U.S., 5, 15–18, 72–73, 82, 97–98; definition of racial identity in, 29; and displacement of black South Africans, 29; and economic issues, 11–12; and education, 87; effects of, 29–30, 85, 106, 110; and family structure, 107–8; and film, 16–17, 105–11; and homogeneity of white identity, 74; images of race and ethnicity in, 117; and language, 18, 109; legacy of, 15–18, 119, 126–27; legalization of, 72; and markings of race, 23–24; origins of, 72; police as embodiment of, 107–8; politics of, 89, 125; and power, 17, 117–18; press role in, 79; and privileging, 12–13, 127; and sexuality, 89; "truths" of, 88; and violence, 12, 15–18, 72–73, 119, 126–27; white liberal denunciation of, 110; white riots' functions in, 20–21; and wit-

nessing white riots, 28–30; women's role in, 27, 89. *See also* South Africa; United States; white supremacy
Appiah, Anthony, 20
Argus (South African newspaper), 82
Asking for Trouble (Woods), 110
Associated Press, 123
Atlanta, Georgia: riots in, 64, 66, 100–101
Attenborough, Richard, 110
attribution, 13

Bakhtin, M. M., 22, 54
Baltimore, Maryland: riots in, 112
Bantu, 17, 29, 76, 78, 82, 106, 107, 108
Bantu Authorities Act (1951), 29
"Bantu-ness," 73–74
Barber, Jesse Max, 64–65
"Benito Cereno" (Melville), 40
Bhabha, Homi, 6
Biko, Stephen, 4, 71, 73–74, 78, 110
Black and White in South East Africa (Evans), 15
black bodies: and apartheid, 17–18, 23, 72–73, 83, 89, 96, 114, 120; apprehension of, 23; blame on, 21; as center of riots, 33–34; construction of, 23–24, 102; and definition of riots, 21; in films, 18, 115, 121; images of, 94, 118, 121, 123; in literature, 18, 85, 91, 104–5; male, 35, 36, 41, 44, 48, 60, 111–15, 120–23; national consciousness centering on, 24; press/media images of, 18, 94; and privileging, 12–13, 127; and race as shaping culture, 3–4; and race in South Africa and U.S., 12–13, 94; and race riots, 5; and racialized ululation, 24–26; seen as aggressors,

politics and race/politics and media (*cont.*)
in Sepamla novel, 84, 85; and Soweto
Uprising, 74–84; and Wilmington Race
Riot, 18, 37, 38, 39–49, 76–77, 98, 101;
and witnessing white riots, 30. *See also*
Democratic Party; Republican Party
Pope, Wesley, 39–40, 43
Populist Movement, 48–49
praise poems, 85–86
President's Initiative on Race (Clinton
administration), 8–9, 11, 117
press: access to, 26; and apartheid, 79; and
blacks as editors, 29, 64–65; censorship of, 29, 74, 75, 79, 84; in Chesnutt's
novel, 52, 53, 63, 64–65; images of blacks
in, 33–34, 39, 41, 44, 46, 79, 94; international, 81, 82; and invisibility of white
riots, 8; and politics of race, 39–49;
power of, 13; and racialized ululation,
7, 25; role in race ideology of, 13–14;
and role of African American literature, 54–55; as self-censuring, 81; in
Sepamla novel, 87–88, 93–94; silencing
of, 91; in South Africa, 29–30, 74, 75,
76, 79–80, 81–83, 84, 91; support for
white supremacy by, 35–36. *See also* black
press; media; writers/reporters; *specific
newspaper, person, riot*
Presumed Guilty (Koon), 122–23
"Prism" (Lorde), 102

Qoboza, Percy, 80

race: Chesnutt's theory about, 4, 72; coding
cultural constructions of, 60–61; and
differences as learned, 37; and gender, 33,
36; markings of, 23–24, 82; mutability of,
53, 56; physical traces of, 100; as shaping
culture, 3–4, 19, 23; as shaping national
contours, 3
race consciousness, 8, 78, 101, 108
race riots: and black bodies, 5; characteristics of, 5; cultural surroundings as
defining, 21; as defining race relations,
4–5; displacement of white riots by, 111;
functions of, 8; and language, 22–23;
and racialized ululation, 25; reasons for,
5; relationship between white riots and,
102–5; student protests as, 7; as threats
to social order, 18; white riots as, 18;
writers/reporters' definition of, 97

racial difference: and blackness, 20
racial hierarchy, 20
racialized ululation: and black press, 27,
28; as call to violence, 8, 24–26, 114; in
Chesnutt novel, 58, 59, 62, 67, 69; in
Coetzee novel, 97; in *Do the Right Thing*,
114–15; in *No Way Out*, 111, 112; and
sanitizing action of police, 83–84; vio-
lently generative power of, 112; white riot
as, 79–81; and witnessing white riots, 30.
See also specific riot
racial purity, 36, 49
racial stereotypes, 16, 52
railroads, 51–53, 66, 84–85, 106–7
Raleigh Times, 39, 43
Rand Daily Mail, 71, 80–81, 82, 83
rape, 28, 32–33, 34–36, 37, 43–44, 60
Reconstruction, 19
Redshirts, 43, 61
Reinhold, Robert, 62
Republican Party, 37, 46, 48–49, 98
Ride on the Whirlwind, A (Sepamla), 8,
84–91, 93–94
Riebeeck, Jan van, 28
"Riot" (Brooks), 102
Riot (film, 1969), 111–12
Riot (film, 1997), 115
riots/rioting: black bodies associated with,
25; and construction of black bodies,
102; as cultural events, 73; cultural lega-
cies of, 118; as culturally constructed
events, 100–102; definition of, 81–82;
in film, 105–15; as initiated by govern-
mental and police agencies, 75; massacre
distinguished from, 37–38; media's
blackening of, 126; as replacement for
lynchings, 98; representative bodies as
center of, 33–34
Roodt, Darrell, 106, 107, 108, 109, 110
Rosewood (film), 115
Rosewood, Florida: riot in, 115
Russwurm, John B., 27

Sadgwar, Carrie, 44
Sadgwar, Frederick, 42
salvation, 21
San/Koi-Khoin, 28, 29
Sarafina! (film), 8, 105–9
Schwarzenegger, Arnold, 121
Sembene, Ousman, 75
Sepamla, Sipho, 8, 84–91, 93–94

Truth, Sojourner, 27
Truth and Reconciliation Commission
(South Africa), 8, 12, 91, 117, 119
"tru-truth," 84, 87, 90, 91
Tulsa, Oklahoma: riots in, 28
Twilight: Los Angeles (Smith), 123

United Nations, 17
United States: as audience for South African
films, 110; black bodies in, 12–13, 94; in
Butler novel, 104–5; connection between
South African cultural experiences and,
3, 5, 7–8, 9, 15–18, 19, 72–73, 82, 95–
96, 97–98; in future, 9, 118; history of
white riots in, 93, 94; Jim Crow in, 50,
51–53, 66, 72; legacy of race in, 104–5;
methods for inscribing race in, 13; official
documents about history of race relations
in, 12; power in, 16; race differences in,
100; silence about South African violence
in, 71; silencing in, 95; Soweto Uprising
as newsworthy in, 82; violence as characteristic of, 126; white privilege in, 4, 12,
126. *See also* apartheid; *specific riot*
urban culture, black, 27, 119
Uys, Fanie, 118–19, 124–25

Vargas, Elizabeth, 125–26
violence: acculturating racial, 15–18; and
apartheid, 12, 15–18, 72–73, 119, 126–27;
and black bodies, 6–7, 18, 22, 72–73, 96,
124; blackening of, 12, 13; and blackness,
5, 7, 20; black-on-black, 24, 82, 102,
126; in Butler novel, 104–5; in Chesnutt
novel, 62, 65–66, 69; desensitization of,
121; in *Do the Right Thing*, 112–15; and
economic issues, 12; in Ellison novel,
101; erasure of white, 111; and international press coverage, 81; language of,
109; and miscegenation, 65; in Morrison
novel, 103; as natural solution to social
problem, 126; as necessary and good, 21;
as political and social necessity, 14; and
privileging, 5, 6, 12, 102, 115, 126; and
race as shaping culture, 4; and racialized
ululation, 21, 24–26; sanctioning of,
6; sexual undertones of racial, 32–33,
122–23; silencing of racial, 96; as treated
according to identity of riot participants,
14–15; and white supremacy, 5, 14. *See*

also weapons; *specific film, literary work,
or riot*
Virginia Union University, 64
Voice of the Negro (black newspaper), 64

Waddell, Alfred Moore, 31, 40, 42, 47, 62,
64
Walfaardt, Alwyn, 118–19, 124–25
Wallace, Christopher "Biggie Smalls," 27
Washington, Booker T., 66, 102
Watts riot (1965), 111–12
weapons, 18–19, 25, 38, 40, 41, 47, 54, 83,
109, 111. *See also* Gatling guns
Wells-Barnett, Ida B., 27–28, 36
Welsh, Frank, 72
West, Cornel, 5, 19
Whannel, Paddy, 120, 126
Wheatley, Phillis, 26
White, Hayden, 30
White, Walter, 100–101, 102
white bodies, 7, 18
white divinity, myth of, 89
white men: as beleaguered minority, 126;
and miscegenation, 21; in Mmabatho of,
123–26
whiteness: definition of, 24
white poverty: blacks blamed for, 43
white privilege: in African American literature, 26, 102; and apartheid, 12–13,
127; and black bodies, 12–13, 117; and
blackness, 6; and black press, 27; in Butler novel, 103, 105; in Chesnutt novel,
60; codification of, 60; and connection
of South African and U.S. cultures, 19;
as defining national culture, 19–20; in
future, 118; language of, 98; as making
race riots out of white riots, 94; Manly
attack on, 44; and Mmabatho, 125, 126;
and racial awakening, 102; and racialized
ululation, 24; in *Sarafina!*, 106, 107; in
Sepamla novel, 89, 94; in South Africa,
4, 12, 73, 74, 78, 83, 94, 105; and Soweto
Uprising, 73, 78, 83, 105; and sustaining
social order, 13; in U.S., 4, 12, 126; and
violence, 5, 6, 12, 102, 115, 126; and white
riots, 4, 18, 26; and white supremacy, 3,
33, 37; and Wilmington Race Riot, 98
white riots: blackening of, 21–22; and
blackness, 5; characteristics of, 5; cultural effects of, 104; definition of, 20;

DATE DUE

JUN 1 1 2003